Spotlight on Language

A teacher's toolkit of instant language activities

Glynis Hannell

Routledge
Taylor & Francis Group

LONDON AND NEW YORK

First published 2009
by Routledge
2 Park Square, Milton Park, Abingdon, Oxon OX14 4RN

Routledge is an imprint of the Taylor & Francis Group, an informa business

© 2009 Glynis Hannell

Typeset in Sabon by
Florence Production Ltd, Stoodleigh, Devon
Printed and bound in Great Britain by
MPG Books Ltd, Bodmin

British Library Cataloguing in Publication Data
A catalogue record for this book is available from the British Library

ISBN10: 0–415–47311–X (pbk)
ISBN13: 978–0–415–47311–8 (pbk)

Contents

Other books from Routledge by Glynis Hannell

Spotlight on Writing: A teacher's toolkit of instant writing activities
978–0–415–47308–8

Spotlight on Reading: A teacher's toolkit of instant reading activities
978–0–415–47307–1

Spotlight on Spelling: A teacher's toolkit of instant spelling activities
978–0–415–47305–7

Spotlight on Your Inclusive Classroom: A teacher's toolkit of instant inclusive activities
978–0–415–47306–4

Success with Inclusion: 1001 Teaching strategies and activities that really work
978–0–415–44534–4

Dyscalculia: Action plans for successful learning in mathematics
978–1–84312–387–3

Dyslexia: Action plans for successful learning
978–1–84312–214–2

Promoting Positive Thinking: Building children's self-esteem, self-confidence and optimism
978–1–84312–257–9

CHAPTER 1

Introduction

Language: an essential for inclusion

Can you imagine living in a world without language? Language really does make the world go around! Almost everything we do depends on language. Just imagine not being able to explain what you want or understand what you are told. Without language life would be very difficult and very dull.

It follows that the more easily pupils can handle both spoken language and internal 'thinking' language, the more effectively they will be able to function in all facets of their lives. In the classroom good language skills help to maximise learning, promote good social development and increase self-confidence and personal satisfaction.

Language difficulties

Without fluent language a child is disadvantaged socially, emotionally, intellectually and educationally. Classrooms are very language-rich environments and language pervades all areas of learning and socialisation. Teachers talk, explain, question, describe and guide using language. Peers exchange ideas, have fun, learn from each other, cooperate and develop friendships through the medium of language.

Pupils who have difficulties with language may find themselves falling behind their peers with learning, because they do not understand all that the teacher says or because they cannot express themselves adequately. Reading comprehension and written expression will be seriously compromised by poor reading skills. Pupils may also be socially marginalised and disadvantaged by poor communication. They may easily develop behavioural problems because of difficulties in understanding and/or being understood.

Your inclusive classroom

Your inclusive classroom will offer an inclusive programme that takes into consideration the needs of pupils with language difficulties, whether these difficulties are due to cultural, developmental, social or other causes. If language difficulties can be addressed, then many related problems, such as loss of confidence, poor learning outcomes and social difficulties, may be avoided.

Language is a complex skill and it follows that many pupils in your classroom will need a high level of effective, inclusive teaching, over an extended period of time, in order to be able to reach a reasonable level of competence.

What is language?

The extraordinary ability to use spoken and written language for communication is unique to the human race. The use of a system of spoken language clearly separates the human species from the rest of the animal kingdom.

Human language is a highly complex communication system, relying on relatively few 'building blocks' of sound to create an infinite number of meanings.

Language is more than just learning the meanings of words. It is fascinating to listen to young children beginning to use language. From their mistakes we can hear how much they have intuitively picked up about formal grammar from the language they have heard around them.

Three-year-old Madison says '*I goed to the park*', demonstrating that she has already worked out that in English we generally use the word ending *ed* to indicate the past tense.

Madison has overgeneralised this rule to apply to the irregular verbs:

> I played, I cooked, I jumped, I goed, I runned

Madison may also have worked out that the *s* indicates a plural. Once again she may overgeneralise this rule at first:

> my dogs, my cats, my sheeps

> two hands, two arms, two feets

The acquisition of language skills is one of the major developmental tasks of childhood. The child's social, intellectual and academic development is closely related to the emergence of language skills.

All language is learnt in a social setting. While informal, incidental learning forms the 'backbone' of most children's language development, explicit, guided language experiences are also important to enable many pupils to maximise their language skills. This book provides a range of activities designed to stimulate appropriate language experiences for all your pupils, so that you can help them to develop their ability to use language in a variety of situations.

There are critical periods in children's development when they are at their most receptive to input. We know that children are at their peak of receptiveness for language input during the first eight or so years of life. Providing appropriate input or stimulation at this stage of development therefore takes advantage of this period of heightened sensitivity. However, language development does, of course, continue to progress throughout childhood and into adulthood and even old age.

There are three main types of language, all interrelated:

- *Receptive language* refers to the pupil's ability to *take in* or *receive* language. This involves not only understanding words, but also understanding the rules of language.

- *Expressive language* refers to the pupil's ability to use language effectively in speaking and writing. Once again this is not simply related to word knowledge, but also includes an ability to work within the rules of language.

- *Internal language* refers to the pupil's ability to use internal or mental language to think, plan and organise. Internal language not only serves as a representation of the real world, but allows the pupil to think in the abstract.

What about speech?

We need to remember that *speech* and *language* are different aspects of the same system. Speech is the ability to produce the sounds that are the building blocks of meaningful language. For a pupil to put their ideas into words a complex chain of events has to occur between the brain and the mouth. This has to occur at speed and in precisely the right sequence for clear speech to be produced.

A child with a *speech difficulty* might have a problem in saying some sounds, or might have trouble with the fluency of language (for instance a stutter). Speech problems can also include difficulties with production, such as being too slow or too fast and cluttered, being too loud or too quiet, or being too flat and expressionless (poor prosody).

Although this book does not specifically address problems in speech production, there are many activities throughout that provide pupils with opportunities to develop clear and fluent speech.

Let us look at how this book, *Spotlight on Language*, connects with the basic building blocks of language and enables you, the teacher, to provide effective, inclusive teaching for all your pupils.

Spotlight on Language: foundations of success

Learning about words

Although language goes far beyond understanding what individual words mean, vocabulary development is an essential part of learning any language. An adequate vocabulary is an important part of both expressive and receptive language. A good vocabulary also makes a significant contribution to mental processes. How much easier is it to talk, listen or think about a topic when you have all the relevant words at your disposal?

As pupils' language skills develop we look for increasing precision in their use of words and an ever-expanding vocabulary. For some pupils, especially those with language or learning difficulties, or with social disadvantage, this process is not so easy. Pupils from homes where English is not spoken may also, of course, be disadvantaged with regard to vocabulary development.

Pupils usually acquire new words quite subconsciously through normal everyday exposure to the language that surrounds them. However, classroom activities can stimulate an interest in words and their meanings and in turn this can increase the pupils' awareness of new words. Acquiring new words improves *expressive*, *receptive* and *internal* language.

Chapter 2 provides targeted classroom activities that can make a substantial contribution to the development of vocabulary. Not only do pupils learn new words, but they learn to *think* about words and, as a result, may become more alert to new words that they encounter day by day.

Language comprehension

Language comprehension depends not only on understanding what words mean, but more importantly on understanding the rules of the language. Some pupils will have difficulties with comprehension (*receptive language*), sometimes finding it hard to make sense of sentences that are lengthy or complex.

To understand and produce language the pupil must be able to manipulate and interpret the order of words in a sentence.

For example, look at these three sentences:

The lion chased the man.

The man chased the lion.

The the man lion chased.

Exactly the same words are used in each of these sentences. It is the order of the words that must be understood before the sentence has any meaning.

Pupils gradually come to understand how word order, word endings and sentence structure create meaning. For example, what is the difference between these two, typical classroom instructions?

> Draw a line down the middle of your page.

> Draw a line to the middle of your page.

Or try these sentences and look at the subtle differences in meaning!

> The boy was the only child able to reach the old gentleman.

> The boy was only a child but he was able to reach the old gentleman.

> The boy was not only able to reach the old gentleman, he also reached the child.

> Only the boy was able to reach the child and the old gentleman.

And so on . . . .

The ability to process complex language accurately is an advanced skill, but one that is very important for full participation in home, school and community.

Chapter 3 provides varied activities to stretch your pupils' *receptive language* skills. However, because every area of language is interconnected, pupils will also have opportunities to develop *internal language (thinking)* and *expressive language* skills as they think about and answer the questions.

Communication

Communication is a complex skill. It involves:

- organising ideas or information into a logical sequence;

- expressing ideas or information clearly so that others can understand;

- understanding what others say and what they want to hear from you;

- constructing a reply that reflects an understanding of the listener's needs.

Communication involves interplay between two or more participants, where each has to take into consideration the needs of the other. The speaker needs to be aware of what the listener needs to know, so that any response cuts out irrelevant information.

Communication involves *receptive language, expressive language* and *internal language.*

Chapter 4 has activities to promote communication skills, particularly in terms of the skills required of a speaker, such as organisation, fluency, clarity and so on.

Language and thinking

The human brain does not just take in information and store it, but manipulates the information in an infinite number of ways in the process we call *thinking*. We can remember, imagine, wonder, invent, guess, deduce, solve, believe, design, work out, dream, conclude, have ideas, make judgements, joke, decide, question, assume, calculate, consider and much, much more. How would we be able to do all this without internal language?

Language can stand in place of objects, actions and ideas, and give pupils amazing mental capacities to do things that they would never be able to achieve by physical means. Language helps to short cut thinking and to deal with abstract ideas.

Intelligence is seen as being very closely linked to language development. Important intellectual processes such as classification, conceptual thinking and problem solving are hard to imagine without the use of language. Good language skills significantly enhance problem solving, creative thinking and concept development.

Chapter 5 offers a range of activities to stimulate your pupils' capacity to use *internal language* to organise and manipulate ideas and concepts.

Phonological awareness

Phonological awareness is the ability to recognise and manipulate the patterns of sound within speech. Many young children do this spontaneously and delight in word plays and rhyming story books, such as *Cat in the Hat* or *Green Eggs and Ham.*

However, because our system of written language is based on the sound patterns of spoken language, phonological awareness is also a very important part of early literacy. Once a pupil can identify sounds in a word and manipulate those sounds, then reading and spelling become much easier.

We know that children who struggle with phonological awareness are at high risk of finding difficulty with reading and writing. Pupils who do not find phonological awareness easy need plenty of explicit teaching and supported practice to become confident and skilled in working with sounds in words. Even pupils who are coping reasonably well with basic phonological skills benefit from learning how to apply those same principles to longer and more difficult words.

Chapter 6 contains activities designed to promote phonological skills.

Effective, inclusive teaching

Let us briefly look at some of the key elements of effective, inclusive teaching.

- Teacher and pupils, talk, explore, discuss and work on language together.

- There are many opportunities for pupils to learn from each other.

- The teacher provides individual assistance when pupils need this.

- Every pupil can participate in the same type of activity.

- Classroom activities are individualised to meet pupils' differing skill levels.

- Extra support and scaffolding are given when pupils need them.

- Stereotypes do not limit individual pupils' opportunities.

- All pupils have the chance to take on new challenges and extend themselves.

- Pupils are taught how to think about language.

- Pupils are taught language and learning strategies.

- Sub-skills of language are taught to all pupils.

- Teaching is explicit and focused.

- Understanding is developed through examples, discussion and explanation.

- All pupils have sufficient practice to master what they have been taught.

- Mistakes or incorrect answers are viewed as valuable teaching opportunities.

- Language activities engage the pupils' interest.

- Activities offer disadvantaged pupils enrichment as well as skills.

Spotlight on Language in your inclusive classroom

Differentiated learning materials for inclusion

Each of the activities in this book is presented at three levels of difficulty. Level 1 is the easiest level, Level 2 intermediate and Level 3 the most difficult. There is deliberate overlap between the three levels to allow for easy transitions between one level and the next.

One activity can be used to suit a wide range of pupils within a mixed ability class. For example, a teacher may use Level 2 for most of the class, but direct the more able pupils to continue on with Level 3 items, while their younger or less able classmates work on Level 1 items. All pupils will be doing exactly the same activity, but at different levels of difficulty.

The gradual increase in difficulty levels and the overlap between levels helps teachers to provide *differentiated learning materials* in their *inclusive* classrooms.

Pupils with language or learning difficulties

The graded difficulty levels within each activity allow the teacher to allocate appropriate *differentiated tasks* to a wide range of pupils, so that everyone can be included in the same activity, at varying levels, according to their ability.

Pupils who experience difficulty with language and/or learning may benefit from introductory work on an easier level than some other pupils. This is often sufficient to prepare them to cope with the more *challenging* items that follow. The teacher can make a decision on whether to:

- provide additional teaching support to help the pupil complete the activity; or

- if the first level is successfully completed, have the pupil progress to the more difficult levels of the same activity; or

- if the first level has only been completed with assistance, have the pupil move to a similar activity, but at the same level of difficulty as before, and provide assistance as required on the new activity.

For example, Ella and Ethan have both completed the first level of *Odd one out* (Activity 17). Ethan coped with this quite easily so the teacher decides that he should stay with *Odd one out* but can now move on to the more challenging second level of this activity.

Ella, however, clearly found Level 1 of *Odd one out* difficult, so she is not yet ready for the more difficult levels that follow. Instead, the teacher moves Ella 'sideways' to Level 1 of *What is the same about?* (Activity 18). The activity provides Ella with *additional practice* at forming categories and relationships between two items. Ella, therefore, has fresh learning materials and a further opportunity to work in the area of language and thinking, but without placing her in a situation where the level of difficulty is too hard for her.

Throughout the book teachers will find opportunities to provide additional input and assistance when this is needed.

A key principle for inclusive teaching is that teachers vary the amount and style of support given to pupils of varying abilities. Pupils with language-related learning difficulties often need *scaffolding*, *support* and *practice* to develop their oral language capacities.

For example, while one pupil may be able to answer a question without any prompts or hints, another may need the teacher to give more scaffolding and assistance such as:

● discussion

● leading questions

● helpful comments, hints or clues

● multiple choice options.

For example, if Dirk is not sure of the opposite of *beautiful*, the teacher might ask '*Do you think it might be "horrible" or "ugly"? Which do you think is the best opposite?*'

The resultant learning is still valid, but has required more structure to achieve the end result.

Pupils with advanced development

Pupils who have advanced language development usually thrive on activities that *challenge* them, but at the same time enjoy being *included* in the class activity. Teachers can readily select a range of activities and/or levels to provide the bright pupil with tasks that will extend their language skills. For example, a very advanced six-year-old might start with Level 2 of the selected activity and even move through to Level 3 if able to do so.

The *open discussion* topics taken from the more difficult levels can be used to promote the advanced pupil's thinking and language skills. The pupil might discuss topics with an adult, or other bright pupils. The more closed questions can be used to extend the pupil's language with the teacher giving *guidance*, *scaffolding* and *support* as required.

Interactive, inclusive and explicit teaching

The activities in this book have all been written as *interactive, inclusive oral language activities*. Spoken language is therefore the main way in which these exciting and varied activities will be presented to your pupils. (See the later note on using the activities as worksheets, p. 12.)

The activities vary in the way they can be handled. For example, in some activities the teacher will ask the pupils closed questions that require very specific responses, such as in *Opposites* (Activity 4). This often leads to *explicit* teaching, where there are definite *right* or *wrong* answers. However, *discussion* is also often generated and the interplay of ideas between teacher and pupils can provide valuable, inclusive learning.

All the activities can generate useful discussion and interaction between pupils and teacher (or helping adult) in a small group or one-to-one setting.

For example, seven-year-old Pippi has been asked to '*Think of the name of something you eat that starts with "m".*' Pippi has given the answer '*Milk*'.

The teacher can acknowledge that Pippi's solution does indeed start with '*m*'. Then further work can be given on listening to the question carefully and checking the answer against '*something you eat*'. Jack may suggest '*But you can't eat milk, you drink it.*' In this way Pippi's teacher can *facilitate* further language development as well as targeted phonological work.

Some activities offer considerable scope for discussion and open-ended answers. For example, all the activities in *Outside the square* (Activity 16 in Chapter 5: Language and thinking) and many activities in other chapters can form the basis of a lively debate and discussion among the pupils. Such *inclusive, interactive discussions* help to promote the development of language and related learning for all your pupils. Teachers may sometimes be pleasantly surprised at how some pupils break existing *stereotypes* of what is expected of them in the ways that they deal with these questions.

Other activities such as *Tell me why (1)* and *(2)* (Activities 12 and 13 in Chapter 4: Communication) not only develop language skills but also provide opportunities for inclusive classroom discussion on topics relating to social issues, general knowledge and practical common sense, involving all pupils making their own unique contributions to the group activity. This generates a shared knowledge and understanding that is of real value in helping all children to experience a sense of belonging to their peer group and indeed their wider community.

Teachers are encouraged to use the activities as the basis for inclusive classroom discussions, which may range across various topics, again stimulated by the activities in the book. These open-ended topics offer many opportunities for teachers to follow through with further development, perhaps in written work or in drama.

Language, the foundation of learning

Learning about language is a lifelong process that can not only provide valuable academic benefits, but can also become a source of endless fascination and delight.

A classroom in which language activities lead to lively discussion, interesting learning and plenty of fun will ensure that your pupils truly enjoy learning about language.

Users' guide to *Spotlight on Language*

Ethical and inclusive teaching

All the language activities in this book have been carefully written to provide teachers with ethical, responsible and inclusive teaching materials. The items promote social responsibility, personal resourcefulness and thoughtfulness towards others.

The use of language related to popular culture (such as superheroes or fantasy), the supernatural, specific religious beliefs or inappropriate role models has been avoided.

Flexibility

Teachers can draw activities from any chapter, in any order according to the needs of a particular group of pupils. For example, a teacher may want to concentrate on phonological awareness and so may use several activities from Chapter 6 in quick succession. Another teacher may be aware that some pupils have limited vocabulary and so may decide to draw on the activities in Chapter 2, 'Learning about words'.

Ease and speed of use

The book is ready for instant use in class oral work. The only preparation required is for the teacher to preselect the appropriate activity for the class, group or individual.

The activities provide a variety of valuable language experiences that can form the basis of a single lesson or series of lessons.

Many activities are also perfect for a quick, intensive burst of language, perhaps to settle the class down or fill in a few minutes before the next lesson.

Teaching notes

The teaching notes at the start of each activity provide teachers with a brief rationale for the activity and practical teaching hints. In some situations suggested correct answers, sample answers and guides are provided for the teacher's convenience.

Suitability for parents or teaching assistants

Teachers may find that parents will welcome the activities in this book for fun-based learning at home. Teaching notes also enable paraprofessionals or even volunteers (such as parents assisting in a learning support programme) to use the activities designated by the pupil's teacher.

Suitability for classroom, small group or individual lessons

The activities in this book all lend themselves to small group or individual lessons, where pupils and teacher work on the items collaboratively. The varied nature of the activities in this book allows teachers to select activities that can form the basis of an individualised programme for a particular pupil or group of pupils with special needs.

All the activities are intended to provide pupils with explicit teaching of the key sub-skills of language. As such they are suitable for pupils with special needs as well as mainstream pupils. The teacher can adjust the degree of individual guidance and support according to the needs of the pupils he or she is working with.

Supplementing a remedial or speech therapy programme

While this book is not intended to provide a programme of intensive language therapy for children with language delay or disorder, many of the activities are similar to those offered in a language therapy programme. Every activity is divided into three levels of increasing difficulty, so that a teacher can differentiate the tasks given to pupils according to their individual needs. The book can therefore support pupils who are experiencing difficulties with language.

Worksheets

All the activities are intended for oral language work. However, the activities can also be used as written language exercises if required. Teachers are given permission to copy any activity for use with the pupils they teach.

Teachers can identify different levels of difficulty, or different volumes of work. For instance, one pupil might be asked to attempt only Level 1, or the teacher might circle the specific items in an activity that the pupil is required to complete. Alternatively, the teacher may set a given number of items to be completed, for example *'Choose any six questions from this sheet.'*

Teachers of pupils with special needs may find it useful to work through the activity with the pupil on one worksheet and then use a clean copy of the worksheet for the pupil to work through the same task again independently.

Making connections

All learning works best if it is connected with other learning. The exchange and cross-fertilisation of emerging skills that occur within a classroom can create a powerful network of interlinked learning.

The activities in this book are specifically directed at language, but teachers will find that they can create links with reading, spelling, written language and other incidental and formal language activities that occur within the classroom.

For example, the class may have worked on *Opposites* (Activity 4), which the teacher can link into a science lesson:

> The paper is very light and it floats, but this stone sinks.
> Will said that the stone is 'not light' and that's a good answer,
> but can anyone tell me another word we could use that is the
> opposite of 'light'?

Follow-on activities

The activities are carefully constructed to provide pupils with appropriate reading activities. Many teachers will find it useful to devise other, similar activities involving current classroom topics, using the activities in this book as a model. For instance, starting with the oral activity of *Opposites* (Activity 4), the teacher might then set the pupils the task of writing sentences that use pairs of opposites within the same sentence.

Approximate age levels

There are no hard and fast rules about which level of activities should be given to children of a particular age. The activities are flexible and open to teachers to use in a variety of ways with a wide range of ages and abilities.

The chart on page 14 gives a guide to the approximate levels usually appropriate for different age ranges and ability levels.

Indication of levels appropriate for given age ranges and ability levels

Age and ability ranges	Level 1	Level 2	Level 3
4 to 5 years			
average for age group	usually		
advanced	possibly	usually	
extremely advanced	possibly	possibly	usually
5 to 6 years			
definite difficulty	usually		
mild difficulty	possibly		
average for age group	possibly		
advanced	possibly	usually	
extremely advanced	possibly	possibly	usually
6 to 8 years			
definite difficulty	possibly		
mild difficulty	possibly	usually	
average for age group	usually	possibly	
advanced		possibly	usually
extremely advanced		possibly	possibly
8 to 10 years			
definite difficulty	usually	possibly	
mild difficulty		possibly	usually
average for age group		usually	possibly
10 years and above			
definite difficulty	usually	possibly	
mild difficulty		possibly	possibly
average for age group		usually	possibly

Key:

usually suitable for age and ability	usually
possibly suitable for age and ability	possibly

CHAPTER 2

Learning about words

Why are words important?

Words are the working tools of language. The more words you have in your vocabulary the easier it is to use language skilfully. With a wide and varied vocabulary you can understand more of what other people say, you can communicate easily, you can read with understanding and you can write expressively. You can also manipulate ideas and think more efficiently if you have the right words as 'working tools'. A good vocabulary can therefore empower pupils to participate successfully in home, school and community. Conversely, an impoverished vocabulary can lead to social and academic limitations for pupils.

Why teach vocabulary?

Unfortunately, many pupils do not reach their potential in terms of vocabulary development. This may be due to lack of appropriate early language experiences through social disadvantage, or lack of quality talking and reading within the family. Hearing, language or developmental difficulties in early childhood can also have a negative impact on vocabulary growth. Some pupils will have a good vocabulary in the language of their family, but have more limited word knowledge in English.

Giving explicit work on vocabulary can often stimulate pupils' interest in learning about words. A 'meta-awareness' of language means that pupils are able to think about language and words, and this in itself can help to build vocabulary. Pupils may notice new words that they hear or read. They may want to ask more about words, think more about words and be more interested in using a wider variety of words themselves.

Understanding word meanings also helps to clarify concepts represented by those words. For example, thinking about the opposite of a word often helps to define that word. Thinking of a list of words that belong in the same category helps to shape the pupils' understanding of that group of words and related concepts. Even the simple task of giving the meaning of a word stretches the pupils' thinking and expressive language skills. How do you explain, for example, what the words *cave* or *catch* really mean?

Vocabulary is usually picked up at random, as children experience language at home and at school. This can work well, provided that the language environment is rich and varied. However, it does leave a lot to chance. Explicit work on vocabulary building in class, using the activities in this chapter, will give all pupils an opportunity to expand their word knowledge.

Activity 1: Word meanings

Teaching notes

Talking about words and their meanings helps to build vocabulary. A good vocabulary is an important foundation for thinking, communication, reading and written language. Pupils will have an opportunity to improve their expressive language as they practise talking about these word meanings.

There are many acceptable ways of defining these words. Sometimes a word may have two or more meanings.

Level 1

1   Something that you use to heat water in.

2   A bend in your arm. Where two bones in your arm join.

3   Not weak. Powerful. Able to carry heavy things.

4   To get hold of something that is moving, like a ball. To get a disease from someone.

5   To move on your hands and knees. To move along on the ground.

6   There is no light.

7   Strong, hard parts of your body. Parts of your skeleton.

8   A machine with wheels that is used to pull equipment.

9   An animal in stories that breathes fire. A fictional animal.

Level 2

1   A natural hollow in a rock, cliff or underground.

2   A carving or model of an animal or a person.

3   A stick of wax with a wick that burns to give light.

4   To give money in return for something.

5   Not limp. Will not bend. Is not flexible.

6   To travel through the air.

7   Not late. Arriving before the right time.

8   A part of the human body that pumps blood.

9   A three-sided shape. A musical instrument that is triangular in shape.

Level 3

1   A liquid food containing meat, fish, vegetables, etc.

2   A large building on a farm for storing grain, hay, machines, animals, etc.

3   A very high part of the earth's surface.

4   Nearly worn out. Not smart. Mean or unkind (a shabby trick).

5   To divide between one or more people. To give someone part of what you have.

6   To jump on one leg.

7   Far beneath the surface (a deep hole). Low sound (a deep voice).

8   Organs of the body, inside the chest, used for breathing.

9   A fight, often between two large groups such as armies or navies.

Activity 1

Word meanings

LEVEL 1

What do these words mean?

1 a kettle _____

2 an elbow _____

3 strong _____

4 to catch _____

5 to crawl _____

6 dark _____

7 bones _____

8 a tractor _____

9 a dragon _____

Activity 1

Word meanings

LEVEL 2

What do these words mean?

1 a cave _____

2 a statue _____

3 a candle _____

4 to pay _____

5 stiff _____

6 to fly _____

7 early _____

8 a heart _____

9 a triangle _____

From: *Spotlight on Language*, Routledge © Glynis Hannell 2009

Activity 1

Word meanings

LEVEL 3

What do these words mean?

1 soup _____

2 a barn _____

3 a mountain _____

4 shabby _____

5 to share _____

6 to hop _____

7 deep _____

8 lungs _____

9 a battle _____

Activity 2: Containers, collections and pieces

Teaching notes

Learning about words commonly used to describe *Containers, collections and pieces* improves understanding of words, increases vocabulary and stimulates thinking. Some of the words are used quite specifically for certain things. For example, *a loaf* or *a gang* immediately suggest a limited range of options. Could you have *a loaf of soap* or *a gang of teachers*?

There are several appropriate answers to many of these items. Here are a few ideas.

Level 1

1 paper

2 bread

3 soup

4 water

5 coffee

6 jam

7 apples

8 stories

9 people

Level 2

1 flowers

2 milk

3 thieves

4 paper

5 books

6 wood

7 cards

8 sand

9 soldiers

Level 3

1 glasses

2 sticks

3 wine

4 lions

5 bells

6 birds

7 names

8 smoke

9 ants

Activity 2

Containers, collections and pieces

LEVEL 1

Complete these phrases.

1 a piece of _____

2 a loaf of _____

3 a bowl of _____

4 a bottle of _____

5 a cup of _____

6 a jar of _____

7 a bag of _____

8 a book of _____

9 a queue of _____

From: *Spotlight on Language*, Routledge © Glynis Hannell 2009

Activity 2

Containers, collections and pieces

LEVEL 2

Complete these phrases.

1   a bunch of   _____

2   a carton of   _____

3   a gang of   _____

4   a roll of   _____

5   a shelf of   _____

6   a block of   _____

7   a pack of   _____

8   a heap of   _____

9   a parade of   _____

   From: *Spotlight on Language*, Routledge © Glynis Hannell 2009

Activity 2

Containers, collections and pieces

LEVEL 3

Complete these phrases.

1 a tray of _____

2 a bundle of _____

3 a cask of _____

4 a den of _____

5 a peal of _____

6 a chorus of _____

7 a directory of _____

8 a wisp of _____

9 a nest of _____

Activity 3: Words in groups

Teaching notes

Learning about *Words in groups* is a good starting point for classification and concept development as pupils have to think of words that belong to the same category. This activity also promotes word-finding abilities. Being able to 'find' a word quickly when it is needed is an important language skill. Word finding is especially important in reading, when the spoken version of each printed word has to be 'found' and pronounced at speed.

A few words are given as examples. There are many more that can be identified. Encourage pupils to think of more unusual words as well as those that first come to mind.

Level 1

1   red, blue, yellow, purple, green, orange

2   cat, dog, fish, mouse

3   car, truck, train, motorcycle, bicycle

4   apple, pear, peach, cherry, banana, pineapple

5   bird, kite, plane, bat, helicopter

6   hat, coat, gloves, scarf, boots, socks

7   house, chair, table, bowl, box, boat

8   vanilla, chocolate, strawberry, mint

9   basin, towel, bath, toothbrush, soap, shampoo

Level 2

1   snake, lion, shark, poisonous jellyfish, bear

2   cow, pig, sheep, duck, chicken

3   pine, oak, beech, palm, cedar, elm

4   saucepan, knife, bowl, mixer, scales

5   Italy, India, China, Canada, Australia

6   book, newspaper, toilet paper, envelope

7   tyrannosaurus rex, triceratops, stegosaurus

8   ballpoint pen, fountain pen, pencil, typewriter

9   shoes, slippers, sandals, boots, socks, clogs

Level 3

1   fish (many types can be named), whale, dolphin, crab

2   bee, wasp, butterfly, moth, beetle, ant

3   sun, moon, earth, Mars, Saturn, Venus, Milky Way

4   brother, sister, mother, father, aunt, uncle, cousin, grandfather

5   stroll, stride, saunter, shuffle, limp, hobble

6   French, Mandarin, Hindi, Indonesian, Swahili

7   hurricane, blizzard, drought, heatwave

8   happiness, sadness, anger, anxiety

9   doctor, nurse, pharmacist, surgeon, therapist

Activity 3

Words in groups

LEVEL 1

How many things can you think of for each group?

1 colours

2 pets

3 vehicles that travel on land

4 fruits

5 things that fly

6 clothes that keep you warm

7 things made of wood

8 ice cream flavours

9 things that you find in a bathroom

Activity 3

Words in groups

LEVEL 2

How many things can you think of for each group?

1 dangerous animals

2 farm animals

3 trees

4 kitchen utensils

5 countries of the world

6 things made of paper

7 dinosaurs

8 writing tools

9 footwear

From: *Spotlight on Language*, Routledge © Glynis Hannell 2009

Activity 3

Words in groups

LEVEL 3

How many things can you think of for each group?

1   sea creatures

2   insects

3   parts of the solar system

4   family relatives

5   ways of walking

6   languages of other countries

7   extreme weather conditions

8   emotions

9   people who help the sick

Activity 4: Opposites

Teaching notes

One way of defining a word is to think of its opposite. What is the opposite of *warm?* Is the best word choice *cool* or *cold?* The ability to use a word and to be aware of its opposite is an important way for pupils to develop their expressive language skills. This same ability enhances reading comprehension and written expression.

Encourage the pupils to 'fine-tune' their answers, as they will sometimes produce an answer that is not exact. For example, they may say the opposite of *tall* is *little* instead of a more precise antonym (opposite) such as *short*.

Level 1

1 little

2 cold

3 short

4 low

5 young

6 slow

7 sad

8 sink

9 light

Level 2

1 early

2 alive

3 far, far away, distant

4 shut, closed

5 in

6 fast, quick

7 ugly

8 wrong, incorrect

9 weak, feeble

Level 3

1 war

2 dishonest, deceitful

3 receive

4 true

5 good

6 cool

7 foolish, silly

8 exit

9 apart

Activity 4

Opposites

LEVEL 1

What is the opposite of each of these words?

1 big   _____

2 hot   _____

3 tall   _____

4 high   _____

5 old   _____

6 fast   _____

7 happy   _____

8 float   _____

9 dark   _____

Activity 4

Opposites

LEVEL 2

What is the opposite of each of these words?

1 late _____

2 dead _____

3 near _____

4 open _____

5 out _____

6 slow _____

7 beautiful _____

8 correct _____

9 strong _____

Activity 4

Opposites

LEVEL 3

What is the opposite of each of these words?

1 peace _____

2 honest _____

3 send _____

4 false _____

5 evil _____

6 warm _____

7 wise _____

8 enter _____

9 together _____

Activity 5: People's jobs

Teaching notes

These words are good examples of how a single word can sum up an entire set of information. The words *dentist* or *chef* give you an instant description of what each person does, without the need for wordy descriptions. The ability to categorise and sort ideas and words is an important thinking skill. It provides an efficient way of dealing with a complex range of details. Knowing the words used to describe various jobs will help pupils with social communication and reading comprehension.

Level 1

1   cook or chef

2   teacher

3   bus driver

4   dentist

5   fireman

6   mailman, postman

7   waiter, waitress

8   zookeeper

9   clown

Level 2

1   jockey

2   pilot

3   mechanic

4   actor

5   travel agent

6   sailor

7   musician

8   miner

9   greengrocer

Level 3

1   plumber

2   cartographer

3   manager

4   pharmacist

5   surgeon

6   journalist

7   judge

8   scientist

9   photographer

Activity 5

People's jobs

LEVEL 1

What do we call a person who . . .?

1 cooks food _____

2 teaches in school _____

3 drives a bus _____

4 fixes people's teeth _____

5 puts out fires _____

6 delivers the mail _____

7 brings food in a
restaurant _____

8 looks after animals
in the zoo _____

9 makes people laugh
at the circus _____

Activity 5

People's jobs

LEVEL 2

What do we call a person who . . .?

1 rides a horse in a race   _____

2 flies an aircraft   _____

3 repairs car engines   _____

4 goes on the stage
in a theatre   _____

5 arranges travel for
people   _____

6 sails a boat   _____

7 plays in a band   _____

8 gets gold from the earth   _____

9 sells fruit and vegetables   _____

From: *Spotlight on Language*, Routledge © Glynis Hannell 2009

Activity 5

People's jobs

LEVEL 3

What do we call a person who . . .?

1   mends pipes and drains   _____

2   draws maps   _____

3   is in charge of a shop   _____

4   makes and sells
     medicine   _____

5   operates on sick people   _____

6   writes newspaper articles   _____

7   sends a criminal to jail   _____

8   experiments to find out
     new things   _____

9   takes photographs   _____

CHAPTER 3

Language comprehension

What is comprehension?

If you cannot *understand* or *comprehend* what is said (or written), you are at a serious disadvantage in every avenue of life. Comprehension of language is a vital foundation for inclusion and in this section of the book you will find activities that will help to build your pupils' skills in understanding complex language.

Our language uses a system of words arranged in an infinite variety of ways. The same words, placed in a different order, can mean quite different things. For example, *John hit Harry* does not mean the same as *Harry hit John*, even though both sentences contain the same three words. Understanding how word order changes the meaning of a sentence is the foundation of comprehension. There are activities throughout this section that give practice in understanding word order.

One of the hallmarks of immature or poorly developed language is that the child relies on short, simple sentences and does not use compound sentences or prepositions (words such as *on, beneath, except, during, after, against*) or conjunctions (words such as *for, and, but, if, then, when*). Without these small words we cannot link words and ideas together in sentences. Learning to work with sentences containing prepositions and

conjunctions, such as those in *Matching sentences* (Activity 10) will help all your pupils to work more comfortably with complex language.

Pupils with learning difficulties are often very unquestioning and will accept whatever is said to them as 'right'. Learning to tell when something does not make sense is a valuable skill, helping pupils to be self-directed and seek further clarification when they receive ambiguous or faulty messages. This skill is practised in *Silly sentences (1)* and *(2)* (Activities 6 and 7) and *True or false?* (Activity 11). Another important skill is to recognise when you do not have the necessary information to respond or give an appropriate answer. This is an often neglected aspect of language development. This is practised in *Listen and think* (Activity 9), where pupils will sometimes have to say that they do not have the right information to enable them to answer the question.

The activities in this chapter give teachers many opportunities to talk about language. Classroom discussion can significantly enhance all pupils' awareness of language and how it 'works'. Teachers can encourage the pupils to transfer their increased understanding into their writing, reading comprehension and general communication.

Activity 6: Silly sentences (1)

Teaching notes

Listening to 'silly' sentences develops listening skills, comprehension and reasoning. Often part of the sentence, for instance *It is dangerous to play in the road . . .*, sounds sensible but the pupils have to listen to and understand the *whole* sentence. The end of this sentence says *because of the tigers*, so the sentence, taken in its entirety, is a silly statement. Apart from building language comprehension skills, *Silly sentences (1)* will help to develop your pupils' ability to be critical listeners, confident enough to question or reject statements that do not make sense.

There are many possibilities and no one answer is 'right', but the following are some suggestions.

Level 1

1   The road is dangerous because of the traffic, not tigers.
2   Swimming pools are filled with water, and water does not catch alight.
3   A bump on your knee is only a little accident. Ambulances are for when you are badly hurt.
4   Sugar, jam and chocolate are bad for your teeth so it is silly to clean your teeth with them.
5   The TV announcer cannot hear you, so you do not need to say 'Goodnight'.
6   You may never learn to swim if you do not go to the pool. A pool is a good place for learning.
7   Children do not put parents to bed. Children cannot go out while their parents are asleep.
8   Goldfish have to be kept in water to stay alive. A pocket cannot hold water or a fish properly.
9   You have to tidy toys up before a visitor arrives.

Level 2

1   It is not *always* dangerous. If you can swim well it may be safe to go into deep water.
2   There is hardly any rain in the desert, so that cannot be the reason why camels like the desert.
3   Firefighters cannot always put out fires. A forest fire destroys trees, even if it is put out later on.
4   You must not taste poisonous things because the poison may make you sick or kill you.
5   Dogs cannot speak so the dog would not be able to ask Jeff to put the TV on.
6   You could still get lost if the path took you the wrong way.
7   The sun sets before midnight.
8   Having homework has no connection with whether you like bananas or not.
9   Teachers have to stay at school until the pupils have left to make sure the pupils are safe.

Level 3

1   There are always 24 hours in a day, all year round.
2   You cannot fall off the world because gravity holds you. The South Pole is not really at the 'bottom' of the world. That is just the way the maps are usually drawn.
3   Sharks are not poisonous even though they are dangerous.
4   Trains have to keep to a timetable so they cannot wait for just one person.
5   It is silly to say 'never'. Sometimes it might be necessary to get up in the middle of the night.
6   Jim was supposed to say 'Thank you'. Sally gave the gift, so she did not need to thank Jim.
7   The answer to the teacher's question was 'Yes' or 'No'. 'Sometimes' does not make sense.
8   There is no point having a car if you leave it in the garage all the time.
9   You cannot go down in both directions, so you have to walk up to reach the town.

Activity 6

Silly sentences (1)

LEVEL 1

What is silly about these sentences?

1 It is dangerous to play in the road because of the tigers.

2 Unless you are careful the swimming pool will catch alight.

3 If you bump your knee you should call the ambulance right away.

4 You can brush your teeth with anything you like, such as sugar, jam or chocolate.

5 When the TV announcer says 'Goodnight', you have to say 'Goodnight' to her.

6 It's a good idea to wait until you know how to swim before you go to the pool.

7 The children put their parents to bed and then went out to a party.

8 You can keep your goldfish in your pocket if you like.

9 Dad said 'Throw all your toys on the floor before grandma arrives.'

From: *Spotlight on Language*, Routledge © Glynis Hannell 2009

Activity 6

Silly sentences (1)

LEVEL 2

What is silly about these sentences?

1   It is always dangerous to go in deep water.

2   Camels live in the desert because they like lots of rain.

3   It is safe to light a fire in the forest because the firefighters will put it out.

4   To check if something is poisonous you have to taste it.

5   Jeff's dog told him to switch the TV on.

6   You will never get lost in a forest if you follow the path.

7   Dad said 'It is past midnight. The sun will soon set.'

8   Sally said 'I do not like bananas because I have homework to do.'

9   The school principal said the teachers could go home before the pupils left.

Activity 6

Silly sentences (1)

LEVEL 3

What is silly about these sentences?

1 There are 24 hours in a day except in wintertime.

2 The South Pole is at the bottom of the world, so you could easily fall off.

3 Poisonous animals can kill you, so be very careful of sharks.

4 If you are late you can phone up the station and ask the train to wait for you.

5 It is never a good idea to get up in the middle of the night.

6 Sally gave Jim a gold watch. Sally said 'Thank you very much for the gold watch.'

7 The teacher said 'Have you finished your work Bill?' Bill answered 'Sometimes'.

8 It is a good idea to leave your car in the garage so that you do not have a crash.

9 If you live at the bottom of the hill below the town you never have to walk uphill.

From: *Spotlight on Language*, Routledge © Glynis Hannell 2009

Activity 7: Silly sentences (2)

Teaching notes

In *Silly Sentences (2)* the pupils have to listen carefully so that they really comprehend the sentences. Then they have to meet the challenge of identifying *why* the sentence does not make sense. Explaining the reasons why the sentences are silly helps to develop expressive language. Your pupils who experience language or learning difficulties will really benefit from this activity, in which they have to analyse the meaning of the sentences and then explain why the sentence does not make sense.

There are many possibilities and no one answer is 'right'. The following are some suggestions.

Level 1

1 Dogs do not eat jelly and strawberries.
2 You do not need your hat on when you eat dinner.
3 It is silly to get things wrong as you will not learn. Teachers want pupils to learn.
4 There is no 'way to the moon', so you cannot give directions.
5 The zoo is not a sensible place to look for a sausage.
6 They should say 'too late' not 'too early'. If you don't hurry you will be late.
7 It is silly for Wilbur to be sad because he won. He would be sad if he had not won.
8 Boots would fill up with water and drag you down and make it hard to swim.
9 Your eyes do not control the lights.

Level 2

1 You could not be talking if you were still asleep.
2 The dog could eat the food if it was on the floor. The floor is a silly place for food.
3 You eat the food and throw away the bag. They have put it the wrong way round.
4 The stamp on the letter went into the envelope, so no one would see it.
5 Having sore feet is not a good reason to put cream on your nose.
6 Writing down your name will not tell anyone how old you are.
7 It is easy to eat honey on toast. It is silly to say it is difficult.
8 Birthdays come in order, so he could not be eleven before he was ten.
9 'Too narrow' means that it was narrower than the door, so it would fit.

Level 3

1 The town and hill are close together, so you could see the town from the hilltop.
2 The food cannot be warm and cold at the same time. It does not make sense.
3 It is silly to move further away, as it is easier to hear someone close by.
4 If they promise not to keep their promises, they will not do what they say.
5 There is no reason for Beth not to like bread because it is dark.
6 Ben makes it sound as if Sam had offered him something other than cake.
7 The choir is a good idea for someone who likes to sing.
8 If Alex was not thirsty he would not want to drink six glasses of water.
9 To hit the ground they would have to fly down, not soar in the sky.

Activity 7

Silly sentences (2)

LEVEL 1

What is silly about these sentences?

1 Give the dog his jelly and strawberries before you go to bed.

2 Put your hat on and then have your dinner.

3 The teacher said 'Make sure you get everything wrong today.'

4 Can you tell me the way to the moon?

5 If you want to find a sausage get a ticket to the zoo.

6 Hurry up or you will be too early.

7 Wilbur was so sad because he had won the prize.

8 It's a good idea to wear your boots when you go swimming.

9 When you close your eyes the lights go out.

Activity 7

Silly sentences (2)

LEVEL 2

What is silly about these sentences?

1 I cannot believe that I am still asleep.

2 Put Dad's lunch on the floor so that the dog will not eat it.

3 Put the food in the bin and eat the bag up immediately.

4 Harry put a stamp on the letter, put the letter in the envelope and posted it.

5 My feet are so sore that I must put some cream on my nose.

6 Write your name down so that I know how old you are.

7 It is too difficult to eat honey on toast.

8 Before he was ten Jack had already had his eleventh birthday.

9 The box was too narrow to fit through the door.

Activity 7

Silly sentences (2)

LEVEL 3

What is silly about these sentences?

1 The town is beside the hill, so you cannot see the town from the top of the hill.

2 Although the food is warm, it is cold.

3 I can't hear what you are saying, so please stand further away.

4 I can promise that I will not keep my promises.

5 It was very dark and so Beth did not like bread.

6 Sam said 'Would you like a cake?' 'I would prefer a cake,' said Ben.

7 If you like to sing you had better not join the choir.

8 Alex drank six glasses of water because he was not thirsty.

9 The birds soared high in the sky until they hit the ground.

From: *Spotlight on Language*, Routledge © Glynis Hannell 2009

Activity 8: Missing words

Teaching notes

In *Missing words* pupils need to be able to anticipate what the whole sentence means, even though one word is missing. The ability to predict missing words on the basis of context is a foundation skill for reading comprehension. For many pupils with special needs this an area that needs particular attention. The pupils' understanding of various sentence structures is also developed in these activities.

There are no 'right' answers, but the word chosen must make sense. The following are some suggestions.

Level 1

1. teeth, face, hands
2. bread, toast
3. cup, bottle, mug
4. beach, sea
5. jumped, hopped
6. all
7. learnt, talked
8. because
9. fix, mend, repair

Level 2

1. trees, pines
2. wished, hoped
3. shells, seaweed
4. pool, beach, lake, river
5. when
6. angry, upset
7. top
8. need, require
9. where

Level 3

1. thank, repay
2. launched
3. beneath, beside, under
4. carried, lifted
5. covered
6. through
7. complete, finish
8. female
9. anxiously, nervously, hopefully

Activity 8

Missing words

LEVEL 1

What is the missing word in each of these sentences?

1 You clean your _____ before you go to bed.

2 'Get two pieces of _____ and make a sandwich,' said Susan.

3 Pour the milk into the _____ for the baby to drink.

4 The children had fun at the _____ when they paddled in the waves.

5 Ben _____ up and down because he was so excited.

6 The little dog ran _____ the way home with his bone.

7 Yesterday at school we _____ about frogs and tadpoles.

8 I went to visit my grandmother _____ she was sick.

9 This box is broken. How can we _____ it?

From: *Spotlight on Language*, Routledge © Glynis Hannell 2009

Activity 8

Missing words

LEVEL 2

What is the missing word in each of these sentences?

1 The tall _____ in the forest made
it very dark.

2 The children _____ they could go
to the circus too.

3 We found lots of _____ on the
beach when the tide was out.

4 It is so hot we should go to the _____
and have a swim.

5 John was very scared _____ he
saw the snake in his bed.

6 Their mother was very _____
when she saw the mess in the kitchen.

7 When they reached the _____ of
the mountain they could see for miles.

8 Plants _____ air and water to
make them grow.

9 'This is _____ we keep our special
toys,' said the teacher.

Activity 8

Missing words

LEVEL 3

What is the missing word in each of these sentences?

1 'However can I _____ you, I am
so grateful?,' said the old gentleman.

2 The scientists _____ the rocket
successfully on Sunday.

3 The gold is buried _____ the
large rock.

4 His team _____ him on their
shoulders at the end of the game.

5 Snow _____ the ground so that
everything was white.

6 The train travelled _____ the
night to get to Milan by morning.

7 You should try to _____ your
homework before Tuesday.

8 There were more male elephants than
_____ elephants in the zoo.

9 The family waited _____ for news
of their son.

From: *Spotlight on Language*, Routledge © Glynis Hannell 2009

Activity 9: Listen and think

Teaching notes

Being able to listen to a sentence and answer a question correctly requires good comprehension of language. This is an essential skill for all students. Knowing when you do not have the required information is important too! Having to say '*I can't tell*' challenges pupils to understand the sentences very accurately. The pupils' responses to *Listen and think* will give the teacher a very useful insight into individual differences and difficulties in language comprehension. Some pupils will probably be relying on guesswork and this will be evident in their difficulties in deciding whether they have enough information to answer the question or not.

Encourage the students to use full sentences for their answers. The following are some sample answers.

Level 1

1   Missy had lost her hat.

2   Puppies like to drink water.

3   The shadows were on the wall.

4   I can't tell.

5   The word 'princess' is only used for a girl.

6   Froggie was in the pond.

7   I can't tell.

8   The donkey was kicked.

9   No, he does not like strawberries best. He likes bananas best.

Level 2

1   Jenna wanted the dog to stop.

2   I can't tell.

3   You will get fruit if you eat your egg.

4   No, Ben did not get caught.

5   No, he had to go immediately.

6   I can't tell.

7   The table was underneath the chair.

8   The word 'shouted' tells you she was angry.

9   I can't tell.

Level 3

1   No, Kyle does not have brown hair, everyone else does.

2   One child got home.

3   I can't tell.

4   Terry is ten because he is a twin, and his brother is ten.

5   The word 'plodded' tells me that Ted was tired.

6   I can't tell.

7   No, Wally did not have a watch.

8   You get into the park if you pay.

9   The girl did the spraying.

Activity 9

Listen and think

LEVEL 1

Answer these questions. Sometimes you will have to say 'I can't tell' because the sentence does not have the information.

1 Missy cried because she had lost her hat. What had Missy lost?

2 Kittens like to drink milk, and puppies like water. What do puppies like to drink?

3 The trees made long shadows on the wall. Where were the shadows?

4 The children were playing in the wood. Was Josh playing in the wood?

5 Princess Pinny played with the bird. Which word tells you that Pinny is a girl?

6 Froggie jumped out of the pond. Where was Froggie before he jumped?

7 Peter went to Mia's birthday party. How old was Mia?

8 The cow kicked the donkey. Who was kicked?

9 Paul's favourite fruit is banana. Does Paul like strawberries best of all?

From: *Spotlight on Language*, Routledge © Glynis Hannell 2009

Activity 9

Listen and think

LEVEL 2

Answer these questions. Sometimes you will have to say 'I can't tell' because the sentence does not have the information.

1   Jenna shouted at the dog to stop. What did Jenna want the dog to do?

2   One little bird fell out of the nest. How many birds were left in the nest?

3   Eat your egg or you will not get fruit. What will you get if you eat your egg?

4   Ben chased the lion and caught it. Did Ben get caught?

5   Sam had to leave immediately. Could Sam wait for his friend?

6   The red apples were in the basket. What colour was the basket?

7   The chair was on the table. What was underneath. The table or the chair?

8   'Stop it,' she shouted. Which word tells you that she was angry?

9   The tigers did not watch the elephant parade. Who watched the parade?

Activity 9

Listen and think

LEVEL 3

Answer these questions. Sometimes you will have to say 'I can't tell' because the sentence does not have the information.

1 Everyone except Kyle has brown hair. Does Kyle have brown hair?

2 She was the only child to get home. How many children got home?

3 They went to the zoo on Thursday. Which animals did they see?

4 Wayne and Terry are twins. Wayne is ten years old. How old is Terry?

5 Ted plodded home in the dark. Which word tells you that Ted was tired?

6 Jake and Barbara threw flour all around the kitchen. Who got hit with flour?

7 Wally remembered that he had not got a watch. Did Wally have a watch?

8 If you do not pay you will not get into the park. What happens if you pay?

9 The girl sprayed water on the boy. Who did the spraying?

Activity 10: Matching sentences

Teaching notes

Matching sentences shows that there are often several ways of saying the same thing. For example *You can stay until it starts to rain* means much the same as *Once it starts to rain you must leave.* On the other hand, *You can stay if it starts to rain* means just the opposite! It can take quite a high level of language comprehension to recognise the similarities and differences between such sentences. Once pupils can understand that the same message can be given in several, quite different ways, they are well on the way to having improved control over the comprehension, speaking and writing of complex language. This is an ability that all pupils need to develop to be able to participate fully in verbal and written communication.

Be prepared to discuss the sentences with the pupils so that they understand how to reason using language.

Level 1

1 different

2 same

3 different

4 same

5 different

6 different

7 same

8 different

9 same

Level 2

1 same

2 different

3 different

4 same

5 different

6 different

7 same

8 different

9 same

Level 3

1 same

2 same

3 different

4 different

5 different

6 different

7 same

8 different

9 different

Activity 10

Matching
sentences

LEVEL 1

Do the two sentences match or do they mean different things?

1 Dogs are very fierce.   Dogs are very kind and gentle.

2 My favourite is popcorn.   I like popcorn best.

3 It is pouring with rain.   The sky is clear.

4 It was very quiet.   There was not a sound to be heard.

5 Freddy was not hungry.   Freddy was starving.

6 Marco was sobbing.   Marco was happy.

7 The cushion is round.   The cushion does not have any corners.

8 It is the coldest time of year.   It is summertime.

9 Jenna was very surprised.   Jenna was amazed.

From: *Spotlight on Language*, Routledge © Glynis Hannell 2009

Activity 10

Matching sentences

LEVEL 2

Do the two sentences match or do they mean different things?

1 Mary and Sue are sisters.

Mary and Sue have the same parents.

2 Sam was exhausted.

Sam wanted to keep running all day.

3 This is a true story.

This is fiction.

4 The water is not safe to drink.

You must boil the water before you drink it.

5 The fire was started by a match.

The cause of the fire was unknown.

6 Sam is six and Ben is eight.

Sam and Ben are twins.

7 Only wild animals lived there.

Tame animals did not live there.

8 It was late at night.

It was almost noon.

9 When Mary arrives you can open it.

You cannot open it until Mary arrives.

From: *Spotlight on Language*, Routledge © Glynis Hannell 2009

Activity 10

Matching sentences

LEVEL 3

Do the two sentences match or do they mean different things?

1 Pat made a statue of a horse.

Pat carved a horse from stone.

2 The lack of water is a problem.

The drought is a concern.

3 The cloth was bleached by the sun.

The cloth was brightly coloured.

4 The decision was unanimous.

Jack and Kate disagreed with the decision.

5 You have to decide by tomorrow.

You must make your mind up within a week.

6 I hardly ever eat mushrooms.

I never eat mushrooms.

7 It is guaranteed to work.

It will not break down or go wrong.

8 It is an annual event.

It is always held every other year.

9 The party was cancelled.

The party was held a week later.

From: *Spotlight on Language*, Routledge © Glynis Hannell 2009

Activity 11: True or false?

Teaching notes

True or false? activities develop accurate listening comprehension. Students are challenged to listen to the complete sentence and then judge if it is entirely true or not. The activities also draw on general knowledge and so help to expand the students' understanding of the world in which they live. The true or false questions make students think about sentences containing prepositions and conjunctions such as *always*, *through*, *unless*, *around*, *than* and *after*.

Be prepared to discuss the sentences with the students. It is useful for reasoning to be explained, so that those students who did not get the right answer gain insight into how to think the logic through.

Level 1

1   false
2   false
3   true
4   false
5   true
6   true
7   false
8   false
9   false

Level 2

1   true
2   false
3   false
4   true
5   true
6   false
7   false
8   false
9   true

Level 3

1   false
2   true
3   true
4   false
5   true
6   false
7   false
8   true
9   false

Activity 11

True or false?

LEVEL 1

Are these sentences true or false?

1 The sun shines at night. _____

2 A cat has nine tails. _____

3 A poodle is a type of dog. _____

4 Babies can crawl faster
than you can walk. _____

5 Every house has at least
one door. _____

6 Vegetables help to keep
you healthy. _____

7 You could run around
the world in a week. _____

8 Monday comes after
Tuesday. _____

9 Bananas and broccoli
are both fruit. _____

From: *Spotlight on Language*, Routledge © Glynis Hannell 2009

Activity 11

True or false?

LEVEL 2

Are these sentences true or false?

1 When water gets very
   cold it freezes and turns
   into ice. _____

2 All animals have four legs. _____

3 Roses, tulips, daisies and
   potatoes are all flowers. _____

4 A square has four straight
   sides. _____

5 You need to keep milk
   in the refrigerator to
   keep it cool. _____

6 A man could lift an
   elephant with one hand. _____

7 You could ride on a cloud. _____

8 Milk is made from cheese. _____

9 Mothers are always older
   than their sons. _____

Activity 11

True or false?

LEVEL 3

Are these sentences true or false?

1 No animal lays eggs. _____

2 Paper can be made from
trees. _____

3 Earth is a planet and it
circles the sun. _____

4 There is an ozone hole
right through the centre
of the earth. _____

5 You are not allowed to
drive a car unless you have
passed a driving test. _____

6 Emerald, ruby and diamond
are all names for colours. _____

7 Neither apples nor potatoes
grow under the ground. _____

8 March does not come between
August and December. _____

9 Your grandfather is your
father's son. _____

CHAPTER 4

Communication

What is communication?

Communication involves a complex interplay of listening and speaking. In their early years children usually become skilled at 'single-track' communication, where they can communicate their own needs, for example saying '*More milk*', or express their own experiences, such as '*I'm playing in the sand.*' These young children can also 'take in' simple communication from others and engage in short exchanges of dialogue, for example responding to '*Do you want toast?*' with a short answer such as '*Yes please*' or '*No thank you.*'

However, as pupils mature they need to acquire increasingly advanced communication skills. They will need to engage in verbal exchanges that involve long sequences of listening and speaking. Pupils must be able to adapt what they say to meet their listeners' needs. They will also need the ability to communicate complex ideas and lengthy sequences of information to others.

Some pupils will find it harder than others to develop good communication skills.

Explicit teaching and guided practice will help these young learners to acquire skills that their peers may have developed with greater ease. Other pupils, already fluent communicators, will still benefit from explicit practice to further develop their skills. The interaction between pupils of varying levels of communication skill will help to enrich all participants' language skills.

Formulating language fluently and accurately is a key skill in communication. Young pupils often tend to use short sentences and then wait for someone else to take a turn. Although turn taking in language is important, being able to sustain language and talk on a topic is another valuable skill that is exercised in this chapter.

There are two *Tell me why* activities (Activities 12 and 13) in this chapter, because being able to 'take in' a question and then formulate an answer in response is at the very heart of good communication. The other two activities work on the pupils' word-generation and sentence-formulation skills, once again essential skills in communication.

Activity 12: Tell me why (1)

Teaching notes

Listening to *Tell me why* sentences develops pupils' listening comprehension of language. Reasoning skills and social awareness are also promoted by this activity. Giving the answers provides pupils with valuable practice in expressive language.

Good answers will probably include some of the concepts given below. There are other ideas that will be equally acceptable. Encourage discussion among the pupils.

Please note that the sample answers given here are abbreviated so that they fit on this page. Your pupils should be asked to formulate full, grammatically correct sentences.

Level 1

1 You cannot swallow large lumps. Chewing begins the digestion process.
2 Gives everyone a chance to cross safely. Makes people take turns.
3 Germs on your hands could get onto food, which could make you sick.
4 Dogs might get lost. Dogs might run into traffic and cause an accident.
5 To show what time they arrived at the car park, or maybe to show they have paid.
6 To help them balance and stop them falling over. To rest on if they get tired.
7 So that rainwater can run away, to avoid flooding.
8 To stop pages getting damaged, and to help the book stand up on a shelf.
9 To keep water in the basin. To save water. So you can get the temperature right.

Level 2

1 Leaves collect sunlight, water and oxygen. Leaves 'breathe' for the tree.
2 Everything is set out so that you can find your way.
3 Bright light can be uncomfortable and damage your eyes.
4 Driving needs skills and judgement that children are too young to learn.
5 Bandages keep out the germs and prevent infection. Stops further injury and pain.
6 Bacteria cannot multiply in very cold conditions so the food stays healthy.
7 New things happen each day and the newspaper tells you about what has happened.
8 Plastic is not absorbent, and towels have to be made of something that absorbs water.
9 Our lungs would fill with water and we would drown. We need to breathe air.

Level 3

1 So that they can communicate with people who speak those languages.
2 The animals cannot survive in the cold weather so they get shelter or go elsewhere.
3 People live near airports and the noise disturbs their sleep.
4 If they cannot deliver the parcel they can bring it back to you.
5 People need to know what is in the food so they can decide if they want to eat it.
6 They decide if the rules have been kept so that neither team can cheat.
7 Daylight is at different times in different parts of the world, so times need to change.
8 Some people are allergic to eggs and peanuts. They get sick if they eat them.
9 Emergencies happen 24 hours a day. Sick people need 24-hour care.

Activity 12

Tell me why (1)

LEVEL 1

Tell me why . . .

1 you have to chew your food before you swallow it

2 busy roads have traffic lights and stop signs

3 you have to wash your hands before you eat

4 dogs have to be on leashes when they are out for a walk

5 people have to get a ticket when they park the car

6 people sometimes have walking sticks

7 there are drains and gutters in the street

8 books have tough covers

9 washbasins and sinks have plugs

Activity 12

Tell me why (1)

LEVEL 2

Tell me why . . .

1 trees have leaves

2 there are maps and street directories

3 people wear sunglasses on a sunny day

4 children are not allowed to drive cars

5 people put a bandage or sticking plaster on a cut finger

6 food is sometimes frozen

7 there is a new edition of the newspaper every day

8 towels are not made of plastic

9 we cannot live underwater

Activity 12

Tell me why (1)

LEVEL 3

Tell me why . . .

1 some people learn to speak another language

2 some animals hibernate or migrate in winter

3 airports are often closed at night

4 you have to put a return address on a parcel

5 labels on food packets list all the ingredients

6 there are umpires or referees at some sports matches

7 different countries are in different time zones

8 some people cannot eat peanuts or eggs

9 most hospitals stay open 24 hours a day

Activity 13: Tell me why (2)

Teaching notes

This is the second *Tell me why* activity. The pupils have to be able to formulate language to explain ideas that are often just taken for granted. This is a good way to develop expressive language and communication.

Make sure that the pupils actually answer the question, rather than talking vaguely about the topic. Good answers will probably include some of the concepts given below. There are other ideas that will be equally acceptable. Encourage discussion among the pupils.

Please note that the sample answers given here are abbreviated so that they fit on this page. Your pupils should be asked to formulate full, grammatically correct sentences.

Level 1

1   Fire can spread very quickly and set things alight. You could burn yourself.
2   Babies cannot walk, or can only walk a little way. Babies can be heavy to carry.
3   The stick could hit someone and hurt them. A stick could cause damage to things.
4   Babies are not old enough to use scissors. They could easily hurt themselves.
5   So that they can reach the leaves high up in the tree.
6   Snakes are poisonous and could bite you. Snakes could be disturbed by humans.
7   It is easier to sleep in the dark. It saves electricity.
8   Elephants are too large to fit into a house. They need big spaces to live in.
9   The dirt from your feet will get on the chair. If someone sits down they will get dirty.

Level 2

1   The road is for traffic. You could get knocked down by a vehicle.
2   The webbing helps to push the water, like flippers, so the duck can swim better.
3   Other people might steal the car, or take things from inside it.
4   It might rain when you go out and the umbrella will keep you dry.
5   The moon does not have air, water or gravity and people need these to live.
6   It is cooler in the shade. The shade protects you from the sun.
7   Medicines can be dangerous. You need to know exactly how much to take.
8   The polar bear will not stand out against the snow. It is camouflaged.
9   So you know how far you have to travel. You might need to get fuel, water or food.

Level 3

1   The things cost the shopkeeper money, so you have to pay them.
2   Cars were not invented. The technology to build cars did not exist.
3   There is not enough room in the streets for everyone to park.
4   There are oceans you could not cross. It is too far.
5   It is very difficult to balance. The rope is too narrow to support your feet easily.
6   It is too cold. There are no houses, shops, doctors, etc. Nothing grows there.
7   Doctors understand about sickness and can often make you well.
8   Pilots need to talk to ground control to get instructions about landing, etc.
9   We need to know the size. We need to know how to wash the clothes.

Activity 13

Tell me why (2)

LEVEL 1

Tell me why . . .

1   it is dangerous to play with fire

2   a baby rides in a pram or pushchair

3   you must not throw sticks

4   babies are not allowed to play with scissors

5   giraffes have very long necks

6   you must keep away from snakes

7   you switch bright lights off when you go to bed

8   you cannot have an elephant for a pet

9   you should not put your feet on chairs

Activity 13

Tell me why (2)

LEVEL 2

Tell me why . . .

1 it is not safe to play in the road

2 ducks have webbed feet

3 people lock their cars at the shopping centre

4 it is sometimes a good idea to take an umbrella when you go out

5 people do not live on the moon

6 people stay in the shade on a hot day

7 you should read the label on medicines very carefully

8 polar bears have white fur

9 road signs tell you the distance to the next town

From: *Spotlight on Language*, Routledge © Glynis Hannell 2009

Activity 13

Tell me why (2)

LEVEL 3

Tell me why . . .

1 you have to pay for the things you get from the shop

2 they did not have cars in the olden days

3 cities need car parks

4 you could not walk around the world

5 it is hard to walk along a tightrope

6 you cannot live at the North Pole

7 you need to see a doctor when you are sick

8 pilots wear headphones when they are flying an aeroplane

9 there are labels sewn on the inside of clothes

Activity 14: Use this word

Teaching notes

Use this word helps to develop verbal fluency and expressive language. Pupils have to formulate grammatically correct sentences containing the target word. This challenges sentence construction and language fluency, especially when more abstract words are used.

There are many possible answers to these items. Encourage pupils to create complex sentences, for example *I wish that I could fly above the trees* instead of *I wish I could fly.* Here are some sample answers.

Level 1

1   The baby laughed at the bird.

2   This is my red train.

3   I use my toothbrush to clean my teeth.

4   We travel on the bus to visit the zoo.

5   I wish that I could fly above the trees.

6   If you want to get to the top of the hill you have to climb.

7   Gold is used to make rings and crowns for kings.

8   The flowers were growing in the garden.

9   I like to swim and I like to ride my bike.

Level 2

1   The fox stole the chickens from the hen house.

2   You can wear a helmet or a hat on your head.

3   There are some tall trees in the forest.

4   It is good to get clean after you have been playing in the mud.

5   Grandfather drove the car all the way to the beach.

6   In the show all the pupils sang the last song.

7   The man shouted loudly for help.

8   The rabbit hid under the shed until the farmer had gone by.

9   They ran across to the other side of the road.

Level 3

1   You can train a parrot to speak.

2   The woman poured the water into the bowl.

3   There was a brilliant light shining in the street.

4   The twins looked alike and wore the same clothes.

5   The two dogs fought over the bone.

6   The fireman lifted the children over the wall.

7   You must move slowly so that you do not frighten the animals.

8   The poor horse was very thin and tired.

9   There were two trees between the houses.

Activity 14

Use this word

LEVEL 1

Use each of these words in a sentence.

1 baby _____

2 my _____

3 toothbrush _____

4 bus _____

5 fly _____

6 climb _____

7 gold _____

8 flowers _____

9 and _____

Activity 14

Use this word

LEVEL 2

Use each of these words in a sentence.

1 fox _____

2 head _____

3 tall _____

4 clean _____

5 drove _____

6 sang _____

7 loudly _____

8 under _____

9 across _____

Activity 14

Use this word

Use each of these words in a sentence.

1 train _____

2 water _____

3 brilliant _____

4 same _____

5 fought _____

6 lifted _____

7 slowly _____

8 thin _____

9 between _____

Activity 15: Two-minute topics

Teaching notes

Talking on *Two-minute topics* helps pupils to create a mental image of the topic. These activities give good practice in expressive language and communication.

For younger or less able pupils you may prefer to ask for *one-minute* talks.

Many pupils will benefit from a few minutes to prepare their two-minute topic before they have to speak.

Good two-minute talks may include some of the following features:

Introduction

Example: 'I am going to talk to you about kittens.'

Definition of the word

Example: 'Photographs are pictures that are taken with a camera.'

Full sentences

Example: 'Kittens are baby cats. They like to play. They look very cute and they are fluffy.' Not 'Kittens are cute . . . and they are baby cats . . . and . . . and fluffy . . . and they play.'

Clear organisation

Example: 'First I am going to tell you how to swim. Then I will talk about animals that are good at swimming.'

Interesting details

Example: 'Bees make special movements to give messages to each other.'

Personal experiences

Example: 'When I broke my arm a nurse helped to look after me.'

Creative ideas

Example: 'I think it would be great to have coloured lights in all the trees in our town.'

References to other learning

Example: 'In maths we used our feet to measure with.'

Brief summary

Example: 'So I think that morning is the best time of day.'

Activity 15

Two-minute topics

LEVEL 1

Talk for TWO MINUTES on this topic.

1 summer

2 kittens

3 hot weather

4 brothers

5 water

6 sand

7 zoos

8 lights

9 bees

Activity 15

Two-minute topics

LEVEL 2

Talk for TWO MINUTES on this topic.

1 photographs

2 teachers

3 your bed

4 dogs

5 biscuits

6 swimming

7 sisters

8 feet

9 cartoons

From: *Spotlight on Language*, Routledge © Glynis Hannell 2009

Activity 15

Two-minute topics

LEVEL 3

Talk for TWO MINUTES on this topic.

1 nurses

2 envelopes

3 the alphabet

4 cold weather

5 umbrellas

6 morning

7 cities

8 clouds

9 autumn

CHAPTER 5

Language and thinking

What is thinking?

What is thinking? Now that is a very big question! Thinking can be described as a mental activity that serves to process information. Together with language, thinking can often stand in place of physical trial and error. We do not have to personally try out six different ways to solve a problem. We can *think* about all the possible solutions, decide which is best and hopefully avoid making some serious mistakes!

Thinking also frees us from the physical, immediate world. We can think of things we have never seen or heard; we can think about things that do not yet exist. We can even think about abstract ideas such as principles, beliefs, theories and so on that have no physical substance.

Can you think about *anything* without also using mental (or even spoken) language as the 'operating system' for your thoughts? Although experts debate the precise role that language plays in thinking, it is certain that good language skills significantly enhance thinking skills.

If a pupil's thinking is based exclusively on their own concrete, physical experiences, learning will have to be totally 'hands on'. Although this is an appropriate way for very young children to learn, it is a cumbersome and slow way of learning for older children. Our pupils who lack good language/thinking skills will be disadvantaged by being 'grounded' in a slower and more primitive way of thinking. Good language skills allow good thinking to occur so that our pupils can fast-track some of their learning and problem solving.

All the activities in this chapter are targeted on developing the crucial link between language and thought. The activities promote the ability to form concepts, discern similarities and differences, test ideas against incoming information and use divergent thinking.

The ability to stand 'outside' your own thinking and evaluate your thinking process objectively (*metacognition*) is the key to good problem solving and logic.

All the pupils in your class, including those with limited language-related thinking abilities, will benefit from classroom discussion about the activities and the solutions to the questions. The sharing of ideas not only provides enrichment but also gives ample opportunity for pupils to observe and talk about *how* to think as well as *what* to think.

Activity 16: Outside the square

Teaching notes

Outside the square questions help to get all pupils thinking divergently. The activities also teach pupils that there are often several, quite different, but equally reasonable ways of finding a solution to a problem. This really benefits the more anxious, less confident pupils who may often hold back, thinking that there will only ever be one correct answer to any question. The ability to think 'outside the square' is the foundation of innovative problem solving. To solve problems we need to use internal 'thinking' language. To explain our ideas to other people we use spoken language.

Encourage the pupils to think of as many unusual and alternative ideas as they can. Keep asking them 'what if' questions. '*What if your first idea did not work? What if you did not have a coat to put over your head . . .?*' Here are some suggested solutions.

Level 1

1 Use a cup, drink through straw, stir it into rice and use a fork, freeze it . . .
2 Use your coat, wait until the rain stops, walk on your hands, use a bag . . .
3 Get someone to carry you, ride your bike or pedal car, put your feet in boxes . . .
4 Use your belt, keep him indoors, close the garden gate, give him a bone . . .
5 Put cheese outside the car, turn the car radio up very loud to frighten the mouse away . . .
6 Put her favourite food in the cage, get a crane and lift the cage over her . . .
7 Tie a balloon to Dad's shirt, use a long string to find your way back . . .
8 Use a broom, use a vacuum cleaner, climb on the table . . .
9 Take the pot to the sink or shower, use a jug, put the pot out in the rain . . .

Level 2

1 Put the bowl inside a bucket and fill them both with water, put the fish in the bath . . .
2 Make a message with pebbles, use lipstick or mud on the window . . .
3 Dig so the hole has shallow sides, fill the hole with water so the dog floats/swims to the top . . .
4 Cut a hole in the fence low down, hard-boil the eggs and throw them, use two ladders . . .
5 Leave the window open, use a big fishing net . . .
6 Make some 'goo' with flour and water, thread a string through the poster . . .
7 Stick newspaper on the window, wear a blindfold, pull the sheet over your head . . .
8 Use a fishing hook and line, take the drain cover off, try a strong magnet . . .
9 Rub flour or cocoa on your skin, wrap yourself in tinfoil . . .

Level 3

1 Float the key in a shoe or bottle, tie the key to a string and throw it . . .
2 Drive and check the car's distance travelled, look at a map and work it out . . .
3 Look on the microwave, television or computer, ask a friend . . .
4 Use a wheelchair, put the dog on a long rope in the garden . . .
5 Put prickles in your shirt, play very loud music . . .
6 Cut squares from the circles, make squares from the triangles . . .
7 Put it inside a book, put it at the bottom of the waste bin . . .
8 Phone from inside the house to a neighbour, climb out of a downstairs window . . .
9 Unpack and wear some of the clothes, get someone to help, use two cases . . .

Activity 16

Outside the square

LEVEL 1

How many ways can you think of to solve these problems?

1 You want to have some soup, but you do not have a spoon.

2 It is raining and you want to keep your head dry, but you have lost your hat.

3 You have to cross some prickly ground, but you do not have any shoes.

4 You have to stop your dog running in the road, but you do not have his lead.

5 You find a mouse in the car and have to get him out without hurting him.

6 The elephant has escaped from her cage and you have to get her back in.

7 The beach is very crowded and you have to make sure you don't get lost.

8 A balloon is stuck high up on the ceiling and you want to get it down.

9 A plant in a pot needs water, but you do not have a watering can or a hose.

From: *Spotlight on Language*, Routledge © Glynis Hannell 2009

Activity 16

Outside the square

LEVEL 2

How many ways can you think of to solve these problems?

1 Your goldfish bowl is leaking water and you do not have a spare bowl.

2 You must leave a message at your friend's house, but you do not have any paper.

3 Your dog has fallen down a deep hole and cannot climb out by himself.

4 You must give your neighbour six eggs, but there is a very high fence between you and the neighbour.

5 A wild bird has flown into your bedroom through an open window.

6 You want to put up a poster, but you have no glue or pins.

7 Your bedroom is too light to sleep in, but you have no curtains or blinds.

8 Dad has dropped his car keys through the small holes of a drain.

9 You have to disguise yourself with what you can find in the kitchen.

From: *Spotlight on Language*, Routledge © Glynis Hannell 2009

Activity 16

Outside the square

LEVEL 3

How many ways can you think of to solve these problems?

1 You have to get a key across a river, but there is no bridge or boat.

2 You need to know how long a road is, but you only have a small ruler.

3 You want to know the time, but your clock and watch have stopped.

4 Your dog needs exercise, but you have broken your leg.

5 You have to keep awake all night. How can you stop falling asleep?

6 You have to cover a square book, but you only have circles and triangles of paper and tiny silver stars. You have glue and scissors.

7 You have to hide £100 somewhere in this room so no one will find it.

8 The front door of the house has locked behind you, but the key is on the outside of the door.

9 You have to take a suitcase full of clothes to an upstairs room, but the case is too heavy for you to carry up the stairs by yourself.

From: *Spotlight on Language*, Routledge © Glynis Hannell 2009

Activity 17: Odd one out

Teaching notes

Being able to spot the *Odd one out* in a group is an important thinking skill. It depends on the pupil using language (spoken or internal) to classify three of the items as belonging to the same group and so find the odd one out. Saying *why* one item is the odd one out further develops classification and thinking skills.

There are suggested solutions given below. However, the pupils may produce alternatives that are equally acceptable. Encourage the pupils to talk about how they chose the odd one out of each set. Discuss the best solution when an alternative is suggested. This activity can generate interesting discussion and encourages *metacognition* (thinking about your own thinking).

Level 1

1	chair	The others are all animals.
2	banana	The others are all birds.
3	big	The others are all colours.
4	train	The others are all vegetables.
5	hat	The others are all musical instruments.
6	sun	The others are all vehicles.
7	dog	The others are all people.
8	sausage	The others are all clothes.
9	flower	The others are all forms of water transport.

Level 2

1	mouse	The others are all people in a family (relatives).
2	river	The others are all animals.
3	school	The others are all things you read.
4	tent	The others are all buildings.
5	teenager	The others are all very young human beings.
6	tail	The others are all coverings for skin.
7	song	The others are all spoken, not sung.
8	submarine	The others all travel through the air.
9	rat	The others are all reptiles.

Level 3

1	paper	The others are all things to write with.
2	silver	The others are all gases.
3	cherry	The others are all vegetables.
4	pencil	The others are all used to build a house.
5	beach	The others are all places where people work.
6	fence	The others are all natural features of the earth.
7	happiness	The others are all negative feelings.
8	draw	The others are all performing arts.
9	eagle	The others are all waterbirds.

Activity 17

Odd one out

LEVEL 1

Which is the odd one out? Why is it the odd one out?

1	dog	cat	chair	mouse
2	seagull	banana	parrot	sparrow
3	big	red	blue	yellow
4	peas	train	beans	broccoli
5	drum	trumpet	guitar	hat
6	car	sun	truck	bus
7	mother	teacher	dog	uncle
8	sausage	sock	coat	shirt
9	boat	ship	flower	canoe

From: *Spotlight on Language*, Routledge © Glynis Hannell 2009

Activity 17

Odd one out

LEVEL 2

Which is the odd one out? Why is it the odd one out?

1 father   brother   sister   mouse

2 river   turtle   frog   hippopotamus

3 book   school   magazine   newspaper

4 house   bungalow   tent   apartment

5 teenager   child   baby   infant

6 tail   hair   fur   feathers

7 story   tale   poem   song

8 helicopter   submarine   aeroplane   rocket

9 rat   lizard   frog   snake

Activity 17

Odd one out

LEVEL 3

Which is the odd one out? Why is it the odd one out?

1 pen   paper   pencil   chalk

2 oxygen   hydrogen   silver   nitrogen

3 spinach   broccoli   cabbage   cherry

4 cement   brick   pencil   wood

5 factory   farm   kitchen   beach

6 cloud   fence   river   ocean

7 anger   jealousy   hatred   happiness

8 dance   draw   sing   act

9 eagle   duck   swan   moorhen

From: *Spotlight on Language*, Routledge © Glynis Hannell 2009

Activity 18: What is the same about?

Teaching notes

The ability to group objects or ideas into categories is an essential thinking skill. Many pupils, especially those with learning difficulties, do not adopt this type of thinking spontaneously. However, with direct instruction and practice they very often 'catch on' quite easily. Once the pupil learns how to look for and identify connections between two words, then abstract thinking has really begun.

Encourage the pupils to use category names, such as *animals* or *flowers*. Concrete descriptions such as *They have both got tails* or *They look pretty* reflect a less advanced level of thinking than classification using categories.

Level 1

1 both animals
2 both flowers
3 both toys
4 both clothes
5 both drinks
6 both numbers
7 you ride them both
8 both girls
9 both rooms

Level 2

1 both open water
2 both groups of trees
3 both reptiles
4 both furniture
5 both entertainment
6 both diseases
7 both colours
8 both countries
9 both feelings

Level 3

1 both even numbers
2 both mined
3 both citrus fruits
4 both gems
5 both bones
6 both precious metals
7 both trees
8 both birds
9 both seasons

Activity 18

What is the same about?

LEVEL 1

What is the same about these pairs of words?

1 dog and cat

2 rose and daffodil

3 doll and ball

4 hat and coat

5 water and milk

6 six and seven

7 bicycle and pony

8 Susan and Mary

9 kitchen and bathroom

Activity 18

What is the same about?

LEVEL 2

What is the same about these pairs of words?

1   ocean and sea

2   wood and forest

3   frog and snake

4   table and chair

5   cinema and theatre

6   influenza and measles

7   scarlet and purple

8   India and Germany

9   tired and hungry

From: *Spotlight on Language*, Routledge © Glynis Hannell 2009

Activity 18

What is the same about?

LEVEL 3

What is the same about these pairs of words?

1 ten and twelve

2 coal and diamonds

3 orange and lemon

4 emeralds and rubies

5 rib and skull

6 silver and gold

7 oak and pine

8 pelicans and penguins

9 spring and autumn

From: *Spotlight on Language*, Routledge © Glynis Hannell 2009

Activity 19: Differences

Teaching notes

The words in *Differences* promote the pupils' thinking skills. Many pupils, particularly those who find learning difficult, do not spontaneously think about words and their precise meanings. As a result these pupils fail to create accurate definitions of words in their own mental 'dictionary'. This really disadvantages them in reading comprehension, writing and general communication. This activity helps to prompt pupils to actually think about word meanings and then helps to 'fine-tune' the pupils' understanding of the words. Explaining the differences really extends the pupils' expressive language skills to provide very accurate descriptions of the differences between the two words.

Encourage discussion. There are often many points of difference between the items.

Level 1

1 Plates are flatter than bowls. Bowls hold more than plates.
2 Trucks are larger than cars and can carry a bigger load.
3 Lamps have something surrounding the light source, but candles do not.
4 Tigers have stripes. Male lions have manes, but male tigers do not.
5 Horses are larger than ponies. Horses do police work and run races, but ponies do not.
6 Leaves are usually green, but flowers are coloured. Flowers turn into seeds, but leaves do not.
7 Boxes are stiff and often square or oblong. Bags are soft and are not usually square.
8 Baths hold water, but showers let the water run away.
9 You can see through windows, but you cannot see through mirrors.

Level 2

1 Sand has bigger grains than mud. Mud can be slippery, while sand is gritty.
2 Jugs hold more than cups. Jugs have a pouring lip, but cups do not.
3 When you doze you sleep for a little while and wake up easily. Sleep is longer and deeper.
4 When you stare you look for a long time, but when you peep you look quickly.
5 Smooth is flat and it could be hard, while soft means you can push it in or bend it easily.
6 When you blink you close both eyes, but when you wink you close one eye.
7 Cold is a lower temperature than cool. Cool is warmer than cold.
8 Girls are younger than women.
9 When you sob you cry, but you make more noise and may take deep breaths.

Level 3

1 When you steal you take something without permission and know it is wrong to do so. When you take something you may think you are allowed to have it.
2 Several is a few more than one or two. Many is a lot more than one or two.
3 Scratching makes a mark on the surface. Snipping cuts off small pieces.
4 Lakes are bigger than ponds.
5 When you laugh you make a noise. When you smile just your lips move.
6 Leaps are as high and as far as you can. Jumps can be smaller movements.
7 Damage means that it has been broken or spoiled. Destroy means that it does not exist any more.
8 Injuries are caused by something happening to you, but diseases are caused by germs or viruses.
9 Violins are played with bows, while guitars are played with the fingers.

Activity 19

Differences

LEVEL 1

What is the difference between these pairs of words?

1 plates and bowls

2 cars and trucks

3 lamps and candles

4 lions and tigers

5 horses and ponies

6 leaves and flowers

7 boxes and bags

8 baths and showers

9 windows and mirrors

From: *Spotlight on Language*, Routledge © Glynis Hannell 2009

Activity 19

Differences

LEVEL 2

What is the difference between these pairs of words?

1 sand and mud

2 jugs and cups

3 to doze and to sleep

4 to peep and to stare

5 soft and smooth

6 to blink and to wink

7 cool and cold

8 girl and woman

9 to cry and to sob

Activity 19

Differences

LEVEL 3

What is the difference between these pairs of words?

1 to take and to steal

2 several and many

3 to scratch and to snip

4 lakes and ponds

5 to smile and to laugh

6 to jump and to leap

7 to damage and to destroy

8 diseases and injuries

9 guitars and violins

Activity 20: Riddles

Teaching notes

To work with the *Riddles* your pupils will first need to understand the language and then take in all the clues. This in itself is a good learning experience for those pupils who do not find it easy to work with complex language. The riddles then stimulate the pupils to use logic and lateral thinking to find a solution. Classroom discussion can give the less able pupils excellent examples of *how* to use language to think things through. This helps the pupils refine their understanding of how to extract information from the clues and make sense of several, sometimes confusing, bits of information. Once pupils have thought of a possible solution, they have to make a mental check to see if their idea fits all the clues that they have been given. It is easy to jump to a conclusion, but checking back through all the known facts is a great exercise in thinking.

Encourage pupils to check their answers against *all* the clues if they have made a mistake. For example, *I am tall. I have a trunk.* could be an elephant. But then the clue says *I also have branches and leaves*, so the answer has to be revised to *tree*.

Level 1

1 tree

2 brush, broom

3 doctor, nurse

4 refrigerator

5 paint

6 whale

7 hair

8 mirror

9 car

Level 2

1 clock

2 ball

3 butterfly

4 glove

5 piano

6 towel

7 rose

8 balloon

9 raindrop

Level 3

1 newspaper

2 coin

3 ice

4 joke

5 horse

6 tree

7 shadow

8 computer

9 sunset

Activity 20

Riddles

LEVEL 1

Who am I?

1 I am tall. I have a trunk. I also have branches and leaves.

2 I help with the cleaning. I have bristles and a handle.

3 I work in a hospital. I can make sick people well.

4 I keep drinks and food cool. You can find me in the kitchen.

5 At first I am wet, but then I dry. I can make patterns and pictures.

6 I can blow water high in the air. I am the biggest animal in the world.

7 I can be straight or curly. I grow all the time. I am on your head.

8 I am made of glass. You can see your own face when you look at me.

9 I have an engine and a steering wheel. Four or five people can ride in me.

From: *Spotlight on Language*, Routledge © Glynis Hannell 2009

Activity 20

Riddles

LEVEL 2

Who am I?

1 I have hands and a face, but I do not smile. I have numbers on my face.

2 I am round or oval. You can kick me, hit me or throw me.

3 I am very colourful. I can fly. I have wings, but I am not a bird.

4 I have fingers, but not toes. I could be made of wool or rubber.

5 I have a lot of keys. My keys are black and white. People play me.

6 I get wet when you get dry. You might find me in the bathroom.

7 I have leaves and beautiful flowers. I smell lovely. I have thorns.

8 I am round and full of air. You have to hold on to my string so I do not fly away.

9 I fall from the sky but I never get hurt. I make puddles. I help things grow.

Activity 20

Riddles

LEVEL 3

Who am I?

1   People read me then throw me away. I am different every day.

2   I am round and made of metal. People sometimes put me into a machine.

3   I am very cold and hard. I can be slippery. I run away when I get warm.

4   I make people laugh. I can be written or I can be said.

5   I am an animal. I have five letters in my name. My name starts with 'h'.

6   I have rings, but they are never gold. People cut me up and burn me.

7   You can see me, but can never pick me up. When the lights go out I vanish.

8   I have a mouse, but it does not squeak. I have a keyboard and a screen.

9   You see me once a day. Before I start it is light. When I have finished it is dark.

Activity 21: Analogies

Teaching notes

To complete the *Analogies* successfully pupils
have to be able to see a relationship within
one pair of words and then apply that idea to
a second pair of words. This depends on
being able think flexibly and transfer
concepts. Some pupils find this type of
thinking difficult and in turn this
disadvantages them in many areas of thinking
and learning. Explicit teaching in how to
identify an underlying concept and then apply
it to another situation will help to equip all
pupils with this important intellectual skill.

The activity promotes analytical and
flexible thinking, which is the underpinning
of many school-based tasks.

Some pupils may not find it easy to
recognise the patterns of logic, so discuss and
explain the reasoning behind the correct
answers. For example, '*You see you use a
spoon for eating, so you have to think what
you use a spade for.*' Giving this type of
instruction can teach pupils *how to think*
using analogies.

Level 1
1 digging
2 dogs
3 vegetables
4 aeroplane
5 red
6 water
7 man
8 foot
9 blue

Level 2
1 animal
2 sink
3 head
4 thirsty
5 windows
6 birds
7 carpenter
8 small
9 kennel

Level 3
1 insect
2 temperature
3 late
4 mother
5 astronaut
6 bread
7 hear
8 solid
9 sad

Activity 21

Analogies

LEVEL 1

Complete these sentences.

1 Spoon is to eating
as spade is to

_____

2 Sing is to birds
as bark is to

_____

3 Daisies are to flowers
as peas are to

_____

4 Driver is to car
as pilot is to

_____

5 Banana is to yellow
as strawberry is to

_____

6 Walking is to land
as swimming is to

_____

7 Mum is to woman
as Dad is to

_____

8 Finger is to hand
as toe is to

_____

9 Grass is to green
as sky is to

_____

From: *Spotlight on Language*, Routledge © Glynis Hannell 2009

Activity 21

Analogies

LEVEL 2

Complete these sentences.

1 Banana is to fruit
as monkey is to   _____

2 Wood is to float
as stone is to   _____

3 Sleeve is to arm
as hat is to   _____

4 Sleep is to tired
as drink is to   _____

5 Carpet is to floor
as curtains are to   _____

6 Fur is to animals
as feathers are to   _____

7 Scissors are to hairdresser
as hammer is to   _____

8 Up is to down
as large is to   _____

9 Bird is to nest
as dog is to   _____

Activity 21

Analogies

LEVEL 3

Complete these sentences.

1 Crocodile is to reptile
as bee is to

_____

2 Clock is to time
as thermometer is to

_____

3 Graceful is to clumsy
as early is to

_____

4 Son is to father
as daughter is to

_____

5 Boat is to sailor
as rocket is to

_____

6 Butcher is to meat
as baker is to

_____

7 Eye is to see
as ear is to

_____

8 Water is to liquid
as ice is to

_____

9 Laugh is to happy
as cry is to

_____

From: *Spotlight on Language*, Routledge © Glynis Hannell 2009

CHAPTER 6

Phonological awareness

What is phonological awareness?

Speech is composed of building blocks of sound called *phonemes*. We can arrange and rearrange these phonemes to create an almost infinite number of words. For example, the sounds in *snip* can be used to create words such as *nips*, *spin*, *pins*, *in*, *sin*, *sip* and so on.

Phonological awareness involves the ability to recognise phonemes and the patterns they make in speech.

Why is phonological awareness so important?

As adults we can easily read a nonsense word such as *unblitting*, simply because we can link letters to sounds and merge those sounds into a spoken word. The reverse is also true. We can hear an unfamiliar spoken word and write down a reasonably accurate version in print.

Many studies show that poor phonological awareness is one of the most common causes of pupils failing to develop good literacy skills. The ability to work with phonemes is therefore an essential foundation for literacy and for inclusion in classroom literacy activities.

Young pupils need to continue to 'fine-tune' their phonological skills throughout the period of time when their literacy skills are becoming firmly established.

Pupils with poorly developed phonological awareness may not understand how individual sounds relate to spoken language. As a result they will have difficulty in:

- learning the relationship between written letters and sounds (phonics);
- blending sounds in reading, perhaps saying the sounds *w-it-ch*, but being unable to relate this string of sounds to the word *witch*;
- breaking words down into the phonemes as a beginning point for spelling; for example, they may be able to say the word *chop* quite clearly, but be unable to work out the sounds *ch-o-p*;
- using existing knowledge of one spelling to produce another, for example taking the word *talk* and knowing how to spell *walk* as well.

Fortunately there is good research evidence to show that phonological awareness is an area of development that responds well to intervention and explicit practice.

The activities in this chapter give the teacher a range of interesting, and sometimes challenging, phonological tasks for the class or individual pupil.

Activity 22: Find the little words

Teaching notes

Find the little words is a quick and easy introductory activity to listening skills. Splitting up compound words is a simple form of syllable division, which is an important phonological skill for reading and spelling. Vocabulary can also be extended through this activity. Teachers should *say* these words (rather than have the pupils read them) as essentially this is a listening exercise.

Encourage the pupils to find both words in the compound words that they hear. Discuss with the pupils how sometimes the two words work together, for example a *toothbrush* is a *brush* for your *teeth*. Also talk about how sometimes the two words do not have any connection, for example *carpet* is made up of two words that do not relate to each other.

Level 1

1 hand + bag

2 tooth + brush

3 car + pet

4 sea + gull

5 pig + let

6 butter + fly

7 snow + ball

8 wind + mill

9 air + port

Level 2

1 for + get

2 arm + chair

3 arm + pit

4 bath + room

5 your + self

6 work + man

7 base + ball

8 ice + berg

9 in + doors

Level 3

1 under + stand

2 scare + crow

3 with + out

4 time + table

5 suit + case

6 day + light

7 hedge + hog

8 earth + quake

9 in + land

Activity 22

Find the little words

LEVEL 1

Can you find two little words in each of these words?

1 handbag _____ _____

2 toothbrush _____ _____

3 carpet _____ _____

4 seagull _____ _____

5 piglet _____ _____

6 butterfly _____ _____

7 snowball _____ _____

8 windmill _____ _____

9 airport _____ _____

Activity 22

Find the little words

LEVEL 2

Can you find two little words in each of these words?

1 forget _____ _____

2 armchair _____ _____

3 armpit _____ _____

4 bathroom _____ _____

5 yourself _____ _____

6 workman _____ _____

7 baseball _____ _____

8 iceberg _____ _____

9 indoors _____ _____

Activity 22

Find the little words

LEVEL 3

Can you find two little words in each of these words?

1   understand   _____   _____

2   scarecrow   _____   _____

3   without   _____   _____

4   timetable   _____   _____

5   suitcase   _____   _____

6   daylight   _____   _____

7   hedgehog   _____   _____

8   earthquake   _____   _____

9   inland   _____   _____

Activity 23: Three words

Teaching notes

Three words is an activity that can really stretch your pupils' ability to think of words that share the same initial letters *and* belong to the same category of word. The activity helps to develop phonological awareness, word finding and vocabulary. This is quite a difficult task, and younger or less able pupils may need help. Teachers can ask for two words instead of three if this suits individual pupils better.

Be sure to give the pupils the sound (not name) of the letters that start the three words. Some suggested solutions are given below. There are other possible answers.

Level 1

1 feet, face, fingers
2 Mary, Michelle, Madison
3 peas, pumpkin, potato
4 goat, gorilla, goose
5 beans, bananas, bread
6 butterfly, bee, beetle
7 Joshua, Jack, John
8 paint, pencil, paper
9 six, seven, seventeen

Level 2

1 hands, hair, head
2 daisy, daffodil, dandelion
3 leopard, lion, llama
4 toast, toffee, tomato
5 lettuce, lawn, leaves
6 towel, toothpaste, toothbrush
7 jeans, jumper, jacket
8 Tom, Tim, Tyson
9 swing, seesaw, slippery dip

Level 3

1 tram, truck, train
2 sausages, sandwiches, spaghetti
3 sun, stars, sunset
4 measles, malaria, mumps
5 Janet, Jennifer, Julie
6 mouse, monkey, moose
7 saucepan, spoon, salt
8 car, cart, carriage
9 stroll, stride, stomp

Activity 23

Three words

LEVEL 1

Can you think of . . .?

1   three parts of your body that start with **f**

2   three girls' names that start with **m**

3   three vegetables that start with **p**

4   three animals that start with **g**

5   three things you eat that start with **b**

6   three bugs that start with **b**

7   three boys' names that start with **j**

8   three things you use at school that start with **p**

9   three numbers that start with **s**

Activity 23

Three words

LEVEL 2

Can you think of . . .?

1 three parts of your body that start with h

2 three flowers that start with d

3 three animals that start with l

4 three things you eat that start with t

5 three things that are green that start with l

6 three things in the bathroom that start with t

7 three things you wear that start with j

8 three boys' names that start with t

9 three things in a playground that start with s

Activity 23

Three words

LEVEL 3

Can you think of . . .?

1   three things that travel that start with t

2   three things you eat that start with S

3   three things in the sky that start with S

4   three illnesses that start with m

5   three girls' names that start with j

6   three animals that start with m

7   three things in the kitchen that start with S

8   three things you can travel in that start with C

9   three ways of walking that start with st

Activity 24: Find a name

Teaching notes

Find a name is a great activity to get pupils thinking about sounds in words. The awareness of sounds in words (phonological awareness) is an important foundation for spelling and reading. This activity also helps to develop word-finding skills, which are important for fluent speech and writing. Thinking about words in categories helps to promote the use of language in organised and clear thinking. Level 1 uses only initial sounds as this is easier for younger or less able pupils.

Be sure to give the pupils the sound (not name) of the letters that start or end the unknown word.

Some suggested solutions are given below. There are other possible answers.

Level 1

1   dog, dingo, dragon, duck
2   milk, milkshake
3   house
4   daisy, daffodil, dahlia
5   stars
6   meat, meal, muffin
7   bus, boat
8   two, ten, twelve, twenty
9   scissors

Level 2

1   red
2   rat, rabbit
3   Josh
4   nurse
5   fruit
6   park
7   light
8   beach
9   sheep

Level 3

1   hammer
2   tiger
3   north
4   small
5   doctor
6   trumpet
7   sandwich
8   ladder
9   sneeze

Activity 24

Find a name

LEVEL 1

Think of a name for . . .

1   an animal that starts with <u>d</u>

2   a drink that starts with <u>m</u>

3   a building that starts with <u>h</u>

4   a flower that starts with <u>d</u>

5   something you see in the sky at
        night that starts with <u>s</u>

6   something you eat that starts with <u>m</u>

7   something you can travel in that starts with <u>b</u>

8   a number that starts with <u>t</u>

9   something you can cut with that starts with <u>s</u>

Activity 24

Find a name

LEVEL 2

Think of a name for . . .

1 a colour that starts with <u>r</u> and ends with <u>d</u>

2 an animal that starts with <u>r</u> and ends with <u>t</u>

3 a boy's name that start with <u>j</u> and ends with <u>sh</u>

4 someone who works in a hospital that starts with <u>n</u> and ends with <u>s</u>

5 something that is good for you to eat that starts with <u>fr</u> and ends with <u>t</u>

6 a place where children can play that starts with <u>p</u> and ends with <u>k</u>

7 something you switch on when it is dark that starts with <u>l</u> and ends with <u>t</u>

8 a place where you go to swim in the sea that starts with <u>b</u> and ends with <u>ch</u>

9 an animal that eats grass that starts with <u>sh</u> and ends with <u>p</u>

Activity 24

Find a name

LEVEL 3

Think of a name for . . .

1   a tool that a carpenter uses that starts with <u>h</u> and ends with <u>er</u>

2   an animal with stripes that starts with <u>t</u> and ends with <u>er</u>

3   a word that is the opposite of <u>south</u> that starts with <u>n</u> and ends with <u>th</u>

4   a word that means the same as <u>little</u> that starts with <u>sm</u> and ends with <u>l</u>

5   someone who helps to make you well that starts with <u>d</u> and ends with <u>or</u>

6   a musical instrument that starts with <u>tr</u> and ends with <u>t</u>

7   something you eat that starts with <u>s</u> and ends with <u>ch</u>

8   something you climb to reach up high that begins with <u>l</u> and ends with <u>er</u>

9   something you do when you have a cold that starts with <u>sn</u> and ends with <u>z</u>

From: *Spotlight on Language*, Routledge © Glynis Hannell 2009

Activity 25: Exchanging sounds

Teaching notes

Exchanging sounds is an excellent exercise for developing phonological awareness. First, the pupil has to recognise the incorrect sound in one of the words. Then that word has to be manipulated to create the correct sequence of sounds.

It is suggested that the teacher reads the words to the pupils (rather than have the pupils read the words themselves). It is very important that all the words are pronounced very clearly.

Encourage the pupils to discuss how the words change. For example, '*It should be dog, not fog. We have to take away the "f" sound and use the "d" sound, then it says "dog" not "fog".*'

Level 1

1 bit/hit

2 fog/dog

3 bike/like

4 tealions/sealions

5 honey/money

6 tick/sick

7 bands/hands

8 glue/blue

9 mitten/kitten

Level 2

1 power/tower

2 bleak/speak

3 lad/loud

4 whales/wheels

5 drain/train

6 hate/heat

7 yearn/learn

8 legs/eggs

9 seal/sail

Level 3

1 clock/click

2 firmer/farmer

3 panted/painted

4 witch/wish

5 shies/shoes

6 brood/bread

7 loves/leaves

8 raisin/reason

9 sorted/salted

Activity 25

Exchanging sounds

LEVEL 1

One word is wrong. Which sound do you need to change to get the right word?

1 I bit a nail with a hammer.

2 The fog barked at the cat.

3 My friend is called Joss, I bike her very much.

4 You can see elephants, tigers and tealions at the zoo.

5 I went shopping and spent all my honey.

6 The doctor came because Sam was tick.

7 You must wash your bands before you eat.

8 The sky is glue and the clouds are white.

9 A baby cat is called a mitten.

From: *Spotlight on Language*, Routledge © Glynis Hannell 2009

Activity 25

Exchanging sounds

LEVEL 2

One word is wrong. Which sound do you need to change to get the right word?

1 The castle had a very tall power with a flag at the top.

2 You must bleak clearly so people can hear you.

3 It was a very lad noise.

4 A car has four whales.

5 The children waited at the station for the six o'clock drain.

6 We used a campfire to hate the water.

7 You go to school so that you can yearn to read.

8 My grandmother keeps chickens so that she can have legs.

9 When the wind is blowing the boats will seal fast.

From: *Spotlight on Language*, Routledge © Glynis Hannell 2009

Activity 25

Exchanging sounds

LEVEL 3

One word is wrong. Which sound do you need to change to get the right word?

1 You can clock your fingers and make a noise.

2 The firmer grows corn for our bread.

3 The artist panted a huge picture of the house.

4 I witch that I could have a dog.

5 If you have muddy shies you will make the floor dirty.

6 I would like some brood and butter with my soup.

7 In autumn the loves will fall off the trees.

8 There is no raisin to be upset.

9 I like sorted nuts better than plain ones.

Activity 26: Rhyming words

Teaching notes

Rhyming words is an essential phonological skill. In this activity the pupils have to be flexible in their thinking and find rhyming words to match the clues. This is a valuable exercise in thinking, word finding and phonological awareness. An ability to find words that fit a given phonological pattern will help your pupils to understand how to use known word patterns to read or spell new, less familiar patterns. Less able pupils often do not make this connection for themselves and explicit teaching may help to bridge the gap for them so that they understand how to perform this short cut for themselves.

Some pupils may need some introductory work to remind them of what rhymes are.

Level 1

1   pear

2   blue

3   rose

4   seven

5   bean

6   fox

7   mouth

8   house

9   coffee

Level 2

1   bike

2   giggle

3   cheese

4   whistle

5   kettle

6   heart

7   card

8   brush

9   plane

Level 3

1   beak

2   snake

3   garden

4   station

5   double

6   stumble

7   juggle

8   shark

9   gale

Activity 26

Rhyming words

LEVEL 1

What is it?

1   It is a fruit that rhymes with <u>bear</u>.

2   It is a colour that rhymes with <u>shoe</u>.

3   It is a flower that rhymes with <u>nose</u>.

4   It is a number that rhymes with <u>heaven</u>.

5   It is a vegetable that rhymes with <u>mean</u>.

6   It is an animal that rhymes with <u>box</u>.

7   It is on your face and it rhymes with <u>south</u>.

8   It is somewhere to live and it rhymes with
    <u>mouse</u>.

9   It something to drink and it rhymes with <u>toffee</u>.

From: *Spotlight on Language*, Routledge © Glynis Hannell 2009

Activity 26

Rhyming words

LEVEL 2

What is it?

1 It is something you ride that rhymes with <u>like</u>.

2 It is a sort of laughing and it rhymes with <u>wiggle</u>.

3 It is made from milk and it rhymes with <u>please</u>.

4 It is a noise you can make and it rhymes with <u>bristle</u>.

5 It makes water hot and it rhymes with <u>settle</u>.

6 This pumps your blood and it rhymes with <u>cart</u>.

7 You can post one of these and it rhymes with <u>hard</u>.

8 You use it for cleaning and it rhymes with <u>rush</u>.

9 It is something that flies and it rhymes with <u>cane</u>.

Activity 26

Rhyming words

LEVEL 3

What is it?

1 It is on a bird's head and it rhymes with <u>weak</u>.

2 It is a reptile and it rhymes with <u>lake</u>.

3 It is somewhere outside that rhymes with <u>pardon</u>.

4 It has platforms and trains and it rhymes with <u>nation</u>.

5 It means you have two and it rhymes with <u>trouble</u>.

6 You nearly fall over and it rhymes with <u>grumble</u>.

7 You throw balls in the air and it rhymes with <u>struggle</u>.

8 It is a dangerous sea creature and it rhymes with <u>dark</u>.

9 It is a very strong wind and it rhymes with <u>whale</u>.

From: *Spotlight on Language*, Routledge © Glynis Hannell 2009